Interval Studies
and Lead Guitar Technique

With Modes, Arpeggios, Practice Scheduling, and Scale Applications

Barrett Tagliarino

To Download Audio, Go To:

monsterguitars.com/isg

The password is "relax"

You will download a zip file containing 114 mp3s. When the book refers to a track number, use the filename with the same number on your listening device. The click track is slightly panned to the left channel, so you can adjust its relative volume somewhat by using your balance control. On examples that include chords, they are panned slightly to the right.

Please help me keep bringing you low-cost quality instruction by posting a review of this book. Your honest rating will help others decide if it's right for them. Thanks!

This redirects to the Amazon review page: monsterguitars.com/ir

About the Author

Barrett Tagliarino is a Los Angeles-based solo artist, session guitarist, and instructor. Since 1989 he has been a full-time faculty member at Musicians Institute, where he teaches core and elective classes in improvisation styles, technique, reading, ear training, and theory. His previous books include *Rhythmic Lead Guitar*, the *Guitar Reading Workbook*, *Chord Tone Soloing*, and the *Guitar Fretboard Workbook*. Barrett's two solo CDs, *Moe's Art* and *Throttle Twister*, showcase his unique approach to composition and life-long addiction to the guitar.

For Barrett's latest instructional materials, recordings, videos, blog posts, performance dates, etc., please visit monsterguitars.com.

Barrett Tagliarino uses Suhr electric and Eastman acoustic guitars, Kaliphoria and Albion amplifiers, D'Addario strings, and Planet Waves accessories.

ISBN-13
978-0-9802353-4-0

ISBN-10
0-9802353-4-0

Contents

Introduction

It's not enough to practice a scale or arpeggio from bottom to top and back. Real music requires that an improvising soloist recall a pattern in any key and position, start on any of its notes, and skip by any amount in either direction within it, applying melodic and rhythmic variations.

Why Practice Interval Studies?

Impatient players may want to stop working with scales before they know how to use them well and instead focus on hot licks that may be hard to apply. It's great to learn licks, but for many reasons licks can distract an aspiring soloist from developing needed skills.

Interval studies are exercises that move through a scale in repeated small melodic patterns. They provide a way to reinforce scale knowledge, continually challenging your ears and fingers to make split-second decisions. They improve technique by making your four fretting fingers and your picking hand rehearse most if not all of the moves they will ever encounter. Repeated practice with the metronome will make your overall technique and timing smooth. They'll also help break the tendency to only move from the current note in a scale to the one above or below it, making your melodies more interesting.

Prerequisites

This book is not extremely advanced but before working with it you should already know:

- basic major and minor chord shapes. We'll review scales and arpeggios before working with them (they're studied extensively in *Guitar Fretboard Workbook*.)

- how to count beats and stay in time with a metronome, and know how various note values (whole, half, quarter, etc.) should sound at a given tempo (*Rhythmic Lead Guitar, Guitar Reading Workbook*).

Learning does not always go straight from A to B, so feel free to skip back and forth in the book. If you're sure something is very familiar, skim over it and move ahead to save time.

Limited Scope

Trying to cover too much in one book can end up with it covering nothing well and confusing the reader. For this book the focus is largely hands-on and technique oriented. Theoretical information is kept brief. Only major scales and modes, pentatonic scales, and blues scales are used.

Working through this book might raise questions for you. Now that I can move around freely within this scale over the most obvious chord, what other chords or progressions or styles can I play it over? How do I phrase rhythmically with it? How about some new scales? If that sounds like you, you may need to next study applications you can find in the other books. On the other hand, if you're coming to it with more experience, then know these exercises will help you acquire the playing chops to support the concepts you've been learning.

Technique Disagreements

There is much discussion and argument about which exact parts of the hand, wrist, and arm should be doing what when playing single notes; especially the picking hand. What follows are just suggestions, based on what has or has not worked for many instructors and students. For every guideline mentioned here, you can find an exception—a player who sounds great doing the opposite—but it is hard to prove whether they sound good **because of** their idiosyncrasy or **in spite of** it. If you really need help understanding something in the book, contact me, but let's not argue any particular technique variation. If it gets exactly the sound you want and does not put much pressure on any joint then it's probably fine.

Anatomy

For clarity these terms are used for skeletal movement.

- Body parts used for playing can be **flexed** or **extended**. For example, you can **flex** the fingers to make a fist, or **extend** them to shake hands.

- Fingers, wrists, and arms can also **adduct** (draw together or toward the body) or **abduct** (move apart or away).

- When the elbows are flexed to play guitar, forearms **pronate** (point the thumbs toward the body) or **supinate** (point them away). We'll say **rotate** for the alternation of these two movements.

- Bringing the thumb and fingers together is **opposition**.

One thing we know with reasonable certainty from athletics is not to stretch a cold muscle. Further, randomized studies have recently shed doubt on the usefulness of holding a stretched position to increase flexibility or strength and prevent injury, depending on the activity. Gently warm up by just slowly playing something easy and then gradually increase the speed and range of motion over the next 10-15 minutes. Playing your first notes of the day slowly to focus on precision rather than speed will also help set the right course for your brain. Any stretching of the wrists or hands should only be done after you're warmed up. Periodically stop playing and move your head, shoulders and back through their range of motion to prevent stiffness and spasm from staying in one position for too long.

About Practice Schedules

Students sometimes ask me to create a schedule telling them what to practice, how many minutes to practice each thing, and how many weeks to keep it on their practice list. I could only do this for you with precision if I watched your every practice session and randomly tested your ability to apply what you've learned. A good teacher will pace either individual or group classes according to the progress made by the students when possible. This means the practice schedules in any book are just rough guides. An instructor can help, but in the end you are always responsible for your own development and retention of material.

Pacing Yourself

When elements of an exercise enter your soloing vocabulary, you know it well enough to retire it from your practice schedule to make room for a new one. On the other hand, **if you forget how to apply it** in your playing, you should revisit or stick with it. Another test for moving ahead is **if later exercises that require prior knowledge seem very hard**. For example, an interval study relies on a scale pattern and the ability to count and play with the metronome. If your scale knowledge or counting or timing are weak, the interval study will be very difficult. Don't let it bother you. Just back up and review the earlier material a little more. Then try moving ahead again a few days later. Basics will be reinforced by any new exercise that incorporates them. Strike a balance between ease and difficulty.

Your first practice schedule might include reminding yourself daily of the boldfaced guides above for moving ahead in your practice. Otherwise, you might forget them and find yourself either repeating stuff you already know when you could be moving ahead, or setting material aside before you really have a handle on it.

The Practice Session

For each new scale or sequence, first work out the best-sounding fingering that is also technically sound, and play through it very slowly a few times. As soon as possible play everything in a steadily-executed division of a metronome click, with your foot tapping quarter notes. **Write down the tempo** at which you were able to play an assignment without a mistake. On the next session, play the exercise cleanly at a slow tempo, then work up to match or exceed the previous day's tempo. Slow and deliberate is the best way to practice. Making a mistake here and there while you're learning is OK; practicing with bad technique or making the same mistake repeatedly is not.

The Big Picture

Do not skip practice days. Make your practice sessions as short as they need to be so that you don't have to skip more than one day per week. If you have more time to practice on the weekend, that's great, but it does not make up for lost days. Skipping practice creates frustrating backslides. A ten-minute session can keep you from forgetting, even if no forward progress is made.

Scales and single-string technique should be only a part of your overall daily practice along with learning songs, rhythm guitar, transcribing, reading, improvisation, harmony and theory, and whatever else you decide is necessary for your own playing goals. 20-30 minutes on each of five topics easily adds up to a 2 hour (or longer) practice session. Use a cooking timer to make sure you don't go overtime.

If you are a beginner, you should only practice for short sessions (maybe just 15 minutes), playing slowly and accurately so that you acquire good technique habits. With time you will be able to cover more material in a session, and the sessions can be longer. New exercises are added each week, while the old ones get covered in less time because you already know them and can now play them faster.

A practice schedule for technique studies is divided among several small items, each of which is practiced for only 1-5 minutes. Multiple short exposures to new information are more effective than fewer longer ones. It's natural to think "I have to get this NOW," but you should resist the impulse to spend more time on one thing in a single session. Let time pass and your mastery of the material will come in due course.

Here, then, is an example of a typical practice schedule and tracking log that evolves from week to week based on self-assessment of your progress. Some things stay on the schedule for several weeks. Others are removed once you think you know them well enough to try later exercises that may depend on them being solid. They should come back on if you change your mind.

Again, this is just an example that includes items we haven't covered yet. You will create your own list. Some items have tempo markings; others say "no click" to show that you can't play them with the metronome yet but will do so in the future. Checkmark completed items to which tempo does not apply.

Sample Weekly Single-String Practice Schedule and Log

	Monday	Tuesday	Wednesday	Thursday	Friday	Saturday	Sunday
Raked Single Notes	✓	✓	✓	✓	✓	✓	✓
Same Fret Different Finger	56	60	72	56	56	60	84
Finger Rolling	no click	no click	50	50	50	56	62
Anchors Away	50	50	54	60	50	60	60
Major scale pattern 1	60	65	70	75	60	75	75
Recite major scale formula	✓	✓	✓	✓	✓	✓	✓
Play five root shapes for C	✓	✓	✓	✓	✓	✓	✓
Recite how interval types change	✓	✓	✓	✓	✓	✓	✓
Define all terms from Unit 11	✓	✓	✓	✓	✓	✓	✓
Major scale Pattern 1 diatonic 3rds	no click	no click	50	56	50	56	60

You can read and study as many units from the book each week as you like, but it's recommended to practice the material in each one for at least two weeks to be sure it has a chance to enter your long-term memory.

Unit 1: Fret-Hand Technique

Some scale patterns cover more than four frets and will require a position shift or stretch, but as a general rule, use one finger per fret. There will be exceptions, like when the ring finger stretches up to play in place of the pinky so that it, in turn, can be used on a higher string. The 4th finger may feel weak at first, but now you should make the commitment to use it just as much as the others.

Objectives here are to:

- avoid injury by keeping the wrist joint in a neutral position (not excessively extended or flexed).

- allow free motion of the fingers.

- keep the fingers on or close to the strings at all times.

- use the minimum amount of fretting pressure required for a good tone.

The thumb should usually be opposite the middle finger, so that the fingers can easily push strings straight into the fretboard. In general, you may oppose with any part of the thumb, but keep the palm off the guitar neck to ensure that the wrist joint is not extended excessively (like when you're doing pushups).

Arch your fret-hand fingers so that each fingertip is ready to touch just one string. Collapsing of the joints nearest the fingertips should only be done for specific purposes we'll be seeing shortly.

It's OK if the thumb tip sticks up above the neck, but if it is very high you may end up grasping the neck like a baseball bat. This restricts the motion of the fretting fingers. The same problem can occur if you point your thumb at the guitar's headstock with the ball flat against the neck.

Conversely, if the thumb is kept very low, you'll have good opposition for the fingers, but depending on the position of the guitar you may flex the wrist joint excessively, which can cause problems with the nerves and tendons that go through it. The placement of your thumb at any time should feel comfortable and help with what you're playing so your hand doesn't fatigue too quickly.

For wide stretches you can pull the thumb lower and point it toward the headstock. The thumb can also reach over the neck to damp unwanted strings on some passages and act as an extra finger to fret some chords. When bending strings you'll hang your thumb over the neck to give your hand an anchor to push against.

These considerations help explain the variation in the heights and angles different players wear their guitars. Wearing the guitar high helps you keep your thumb low so you can play jazzy chords and wide interval skips. Slinging the guitar lower lets you bring the thumb up to oppose the fingers for string-bending licks and facilitates closer string damping. Choose a height that lets you keep your fret-hand wrist straight most of the time. If you play both sitting and standing, consider setting your strap length so that the guitar's height stays the same either way. If you play without a pick try a classical-type posture where the strings cross your body at an angle, allowing both wrists to stay straighter.

If you feel pain, do not disregard it. Stop, rest, think about why the pain exists, and consider changing your approach. If the pain continues no matter what you do, consult a doctor.

Track 1 Light Fretting Pressure

Steadily and firmly pick any one string. The picking force for this exercise is essentially unrelated to the fretting force. With a straight wrist, and your thumb centered with the palm off the neck, gradually apply a fingertip to the string, right behind a fret wire, increasing the pressure just until the note sounds clearly with no buzz. You may be surprised at how little force is required. Pressing too hard will waste energy, slow you down, and also possibly push the note out of tune. Try the exercise with each of the four fingers alone or in any combination: 1 & 2 together on the same string, 2 & 3 together, etc.

Make sure you only press the string straight in toward the fretboard and do not push or pull it in any other direction. The string should stay as straight as possible unless you are bending it on purpose.

Keep your fingers on or close to the strings at all times, only moving them enough to get from one place to the next. Play this and all the basic technique exercises slowly so that you can make sure your fingers barely leave the strings between notes. When you play faster, the fingers need to come a little higher off the strings between notes, and the velocity makes you fret with greater force. Too much of this will slow you down and mess with your tone. Starting slow and making a habit of light pressure and keeping your fingers close helps you keep everything under control.

Unit 2: Fret-Hand Damping

It's said that some players have good tone in their hands. Much of this is really the absence of unwanted sounds. Along with accurately fretting only the notes you want by keeping your fingers arched, you eliminate open-string sounds by damping with the unused parts of both hands. The fretting hand, and its index finger in particular, are good for damping strings closer to the floor than the one you are playing. Even when you are already using the index finger to fret a note, you can flatten it just enough that its inner surface damps the higher strings.

Track 2 Clash with Open Strings

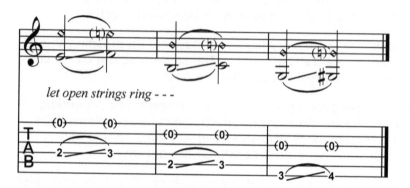

let open strings ring - - -

Play each note shown, first with no fret-hand damping. Keep your fingers arched so that only the indicated string is touched for this first part of the exercise. If your guitar is in tune and the strings are not dead, an open string should vibrate sympathetically with the note you are playing. When you then slide your note up by one fret, you will hear a clash between it and the ringing open string. This is the sound we are going to work to prevent (although on some parts it can add character).

Track 2 continued, Preventing Open String Clash

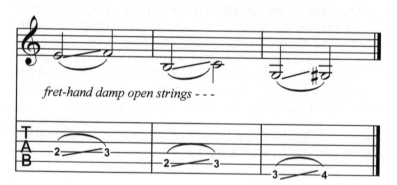

fret-hand damp open strings - - -

Now play the same notes, but collapse your index finger just enough to damp the open strings closer to the floor. The immediately-neighboring lower string can be damped by the upper edge of the fretting finger as well. In the first measure of this example, the index finger frets a note on string 4 while damping strings 3, 2, and 1. Its upper edge also damps string 5.

Any time the picking hand is too busy to damp strings, you'll rely on the fret-hand fingers to damp **all** the strings above and below the one you are on. Overall, the two hands should work together to keep unwanted sounds in check as much as possible.

Track 3 Raked Single Notes

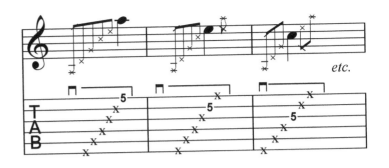

This exercise has you fret-hand damping all the strings except the one that's sounding. Fret a note on one string and damp the other five by laying down your fret-hand fingers. The unfretted strings are farther off the fretboard than the one you are fretting, so you can damp them with the fingers either in front of or behind the note you are playing.

Strum all six strings with a single downstroke (the rectangular mark) of your pick. Let the one fretted string ring out for a full beat at a slow tempo. The other five strings should emit a damped scratching sound with no sustain. Damping a string in two places (e.g. with part of the fretting finger plus another finger) will ensure that no harmonic overtones come out. Do this exercise for notes on each of the six strings with each of the four fret-hand fingers, then repeat the process using **upstrokes** of the pick.

Working on your fret-hand damping separately like this, using long notes, will help those notes sustain longer and project with a clear tone. When you're playing faster, the picking hand will take over some of the string-damping duties.

Unit 3: Clean String Changes

You'll need to coordinate movements within the fretting hand to make sure only one note sounds when moving from one string to another. Along with the attack of a note on a new string, simultaneously release the pressure on the previous string to prevent notes from overlapping. Avoid gaps between notes unless you're intentionally playing *staccato* (separated) tones.

Track 4 Seamless Connection

Set your metronome to 50 bpm and play two notes per click in strict time for this short string-switching example. Listen for gaps and overlaps as you move from one string to another.

There will be many times when you will follow a note with another one on a different string but the same fret. This can be hard to play cleanly. If you lift one fingertip up and put it down on another string, there will be a gap between the notes during the time your finger is in transit, and the still-vibrating string might sound its unwanted open note during that time. If instead you let one finger collapse into a barre, you get the sound of both notes ringing as a chord, which disrupts the melodic line.

There are two ways to deal with this situation: finger-switching and finger-rolling. Both require extensive practice, because you have to plan at least one note ahead.

Finger-Switching

Finger-switching is a very clean way to connect notes without a glitch. For this, **avoid using the same finger for a different string**, regardless of which fret the next note is on. For the specific situation mentioned, assume you have two notes on the 5th fret, on adjacent strings. Play the lower-sounding note with the index finger, then the higher one with the middle finger. This order is preferred, but the opposite order will sometimes be necessary.

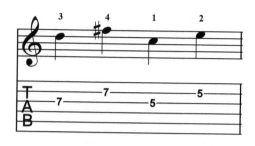

The same notes might need to be played with fingers 2 and 3, or fingers 3 and 4, depending on what came before and what's coming next.

This classical-based technique helps maintain proper fret-hand posture, with the fingers curled over the fretboard, ready to attack notes efficiently. It gives you clean, solid-sounding tones. Applying it to the examples later in the program will teach you to **plan ahead** for proper execution of notes that are coming up.

Here's an exercise to practice and develop the finger-switching reflex. It's not a lick or a melody; it just drills the movement. Play in steady time with the metronome, starting with one note per click at 50 beats per minute or slower. Only increase the tempo when the sound is clear and you feel relaxed while still performing accurately. Record your tempo each day in a practice log. To save space only two string sets (3-2, 2-1) are written; you can add the others as you get used to the exercise.

Track 5 Same Fret, Different Finger

Consider applying this method extensively before moving to the next one.

Unit 4: Finger-Rolling

For the other method of moving from string to string on the same fret, play the lower-pitched note with the finger tip, and then roll the finger over by relaxing the distal joint, to play the higher note with the pad of the finger. The tip should roll off and damp the lower note so that **only** the higher one is now heard.

When rolling the same notes in the opposite order, you have to plan ahead by fretting the higher-sounding note with exact placement of the finger pad, so that the tip will play the lower note after you flex the joint. The finger pad rolls **off** of the higher note. The two notes should not ring together as a chord.

At first finger-rolling may be difficult, and you might end up moving your entire hand to get the finger to fret the next string while damping the previous one. Work on minimizing that rocking hand motion in the next little finger-rolling exercise. It doesn't use a scale or any musical concept; it just rolls all four fingers. Sometimes you'll be able to press the 3rd finger on top of the 4th to help it flatten into position.

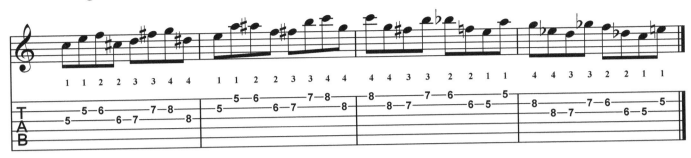

With practice, you'll learn to relax the distal joint in a way that allows the pad to smoothly fret the string. When you're finished with notes that require this technique, return your fingers to the curved posture, taking into account the considerations in the next section.

Unit 5: Pick-Hand Technique

For all the exercises in this book, use alternate picking at first. When you listen closely to your recorded playing you'll notice that alternate-picked notes have better timing than those produced by other methods. Alternate picking gets you in the groove, so make it your foundation. The idea is simple at first. Just pick down and up, all the time, even when switching or skipping strings. Later it won't be so easy: during slides, hammer-ons, pull-offs, and syncopated rhythms, the alternation scheme should continue without striking strings. It's important to develop the ability to alternate pick now, before adding these complications.

First work on an accurate but relaxed pick-hand stroke. Modify it later to include pick-hand damping and muting.

A good picking motion is a combination of forearm rotation (like turning a key in a lock), slight wrist flexion and extension (like knocking on a door), and a small amount of movement in the thumb and first finger, mostly for setting the pick angle to produce the desired tone.

The Thumb and Fingers

Hold the pick between your thumb and the side of your curled index finger. Most players don't hold it on the pad where the fingerprint pattern is. Let the pick point stick out about 3/8" (1 cm). Gently curl your other fingers in against the index finger to support its opposition to the thumb. With this posture, fingers 2, 3, and 4 are out of the way of the strings but still close by and ready to pluck notes. You'll generally avoid making a tight fist or fanning your fingers out, with some exceptions.

It's okay to let the nail side of the fingers glide across the pickguard a bit when playing on the higher strings, but try to keep the shape and angle of the hand basically the same for each string, using larger movements of the arm to bring the hand into position rather than using thumb and fingers to reach for strings with the pick.

Usually just bringing the thumb and finger together and holding the wrist straight over the strings places the pick at an angle that produces a nice tone. Sometimes you may have to flex the thumb a little bit. When angled enough, the pick glides smoothly through the string without getting held back. It's about 30 degrees, but don't think of it as visual measurement. You really judge by the sound and feel. A larger angle between pick and string allows you to play more easily but also introduces scratchier tone on wound strings. Find the pick angle that suits your sonic taste on your equipment.

A significant minority of players hold their picks at the opposite angle from others, extending the thumb so that the edge of the pick nearest the bridge strikes the string on the downstroke. This is sometimes called the George Benson picking style. It does allow for an efficient mechanical stroke where the pick cuts smoothly and quietly like a propeller blade on the end of a spinning shaft (your forearm), but it may make hybrid-picking and artificial harmonics more difficult. There is also potential for injury if the position of your guitar requires you to hyperextend your thumb in order to pick this way.

The Wrist and Arm

A wrist joint can move in four basic directions: up and down if your palm is facing the floor (extension and flexion), and side to side (adduction and abduction). Wrist extension and flexion helps you jump over strings without hitting them.

Avoid excessive wrist adduction and abduction (side-to-side movement), like you'd get if you held your arm flat and still on a table and moved only your palm back and forth like a small windshield wiper. It feels okay at first and is good for control at slow tempos, but when you start playing faster this way you may tend to tighten up and tire quickly.

For powerful picking action with endurance and accuracy, the forearm **rotates** (alternates between supination for downstrokes and pronation for upstrokes) as when you're turning a key in a door lock. This is where the main picking force should usually be felt. You can feel the biceps muscle in your upper arm contract on the upstrokes.

Flex and extend the elbow joint to move the forearm so that the hand is positioned over each string to do the actual picking; most of the better players do not use isolated elbow motion for individual pick strokes or chord strums. The upper arm will move slightly (rotating the shoulder joint) as you move the hand into position. Excessive pressure of the arm on the guitar's top can create friction that impedes this positioning movement.

Keep the top of the shoulder down in a relaxed position. The rest of your body should be in an upright and firm (but not tense) posture that provides a solid base and lets you breathe fully and freely.

Track 7 Forearm Rotation

Practice isolating forearm rotation to replace the wrist adduction habit. It can take many weeks to get comfortable with it, and you'll have to brush up on it frequently. You can apply it to any scale or lick you know by playing with no pick-hand muting. Make sure that your picking hand is completely off the guitar's face, and go very slowly to be sure the wrist and elbow joints are only used to move the hand into position for each string. The rotating forearm makes the actual down- and upstrokes. When picking faster it'll look like the elbow and wrist flexion are part of the pick stroke when you switch strings, but (in your mind at least) those movements are separate.

Unit 6: Pick-Hand Efficiency

Stay Loose

Excess opposing muscle tension leads to fatigue, and can make your playing sound stiff. The more you can relax the muscle that is opposite the one that is contracting while still maintaining control, the easier your picking action will be. Since the two or more muscles involved in any motion are not always easy to control independently, you should just try to stay as relaxed as possible. Think of an Olympic runner staying loose yet maintaining posture and technique.

If you feel the muscles in your forearm tightening up, it may be because you're forcing yourself to play faster than you are ready to, or using too much wrist ad- and abduction. Stop playing and relax, then start again, but more slowly. Pay attention to how both arms and your entire body feel. Do not disregard tension or pain. Nearly all students who want to build speed experience tendinitis at some point, usually from trying to push themselves too hard. Your first goal should be to continue to play without injury for the rest of your life. After that come accuracy, a solid tone, and finally, speed; not for its own sake but to broaden your palette of musical options.

Track 8 Loose Scratch-to-Pick

Damp all six strings with your fretting hand and strum them in time with the metronome, spinning your forearm like you're shaking water off your picking hand. Flex your wrist so that the rotating forearm lets you easily scratch all six damped strings. For single notes we'll try to keep that relaxed feeling and adjust the wrist flex to bring the hand in closer. For this exercise you will not touch the bridge of the guitar or do any pick-hand damping at all. Keep your fingers curled in and your palm off the bridge. We're working on a balance between picking accuracy and muscle relaxation.

After three beats of down and up scratching, keep the forearm rotating in rhythm during the beat of silence as you prepare to make a smaller stroke on only one string. The fretting hand damps all five strings except the one you are playing, for insurance. Maintain the same relaxed feeling as you play three down- and upstrokes on that string. Use a consistent stroke size on each of the six strings, especially the 1st and 6th.

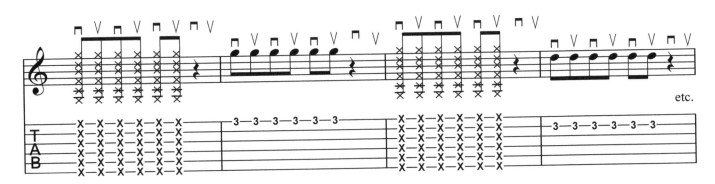

Avoid Anchors

Examples of anchoring are planting fingertips on the face of the guitar below the strings or the ball of the thumb above the bridge. For thumb- and finger-picking like Merle Travis or Chet Atkins, a pinky anchor can be useful because for that technique the hand is stationary. When you're using a pick to play lines, however, a hand anchor interferes with the ability to move into position as you switch strings. Instead touch your forearm near the elbow on the upper edge of the guitar's body. This the only anchor point, and even it should have only a gentle pressure to avoid inflicting nerve damage over the years. The palm's contact with the strings near the bridge for damping and muting (covered next) should not feel like an anchor. If it does, you're likely using wrist adduction/abduction.

Students were noted to improve their sound by working to remove the anchor. Stop working on it and the anchor comes back, sloppy playing returns; evidence that it's worth a bit of vigilance.

Track 9 Anchors Away

This short exercise is designed to encourage forearm rotation and keep your hand from collapsing onto the guitar's face. You'll switch from playing a few single-string notes to strumming a 5- or 6-string chord, keeping things loose yet striving for accuracy. It's OK to let your fingernails touch the pickguard a bit as you play the single notes, but don't anchor your fingertips on it. Go slowly and make sure that you can hear every note cleanly but with no open strings ringing.

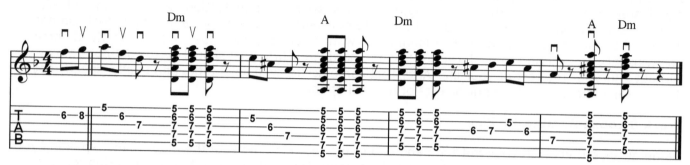

Alternate-pick all notes and chords except where indicated.

Unit 7: Pick-Hand Damping and Muting

When relaxed alternate picking across the strings is combined with pick-hand damping and/or muting, it looks like the hand is slightly bouncing up and down on the bridge, so that only one string at a time is struck. Looking at it, however, does not do much good. It's done by feel.

For our discussions, let's say *damping* means to kill a sound entirely or to prevent an unintended one, and *muting* is when you want a note to be played but ring in a subdued way and/or die out quickly. You can use the heel of the picking-hand palm to get any desired amount of muting, from freely ringing notes bright with overtones to completely dark deadened thumps. Start by resting it on the bridge of the guitar right where the strings cross. Move it in toward the fretboard for more muting. By moving the palm edge up you can mute the low strings while letting the high ones ring.

Track 10 Palm Damping

Play each note indicated, first with no damping or muting. If your guitar is in tune and the strings are not dead, an open string will vibrate sympathetically with the note you are playing. When you then slide your note up by one fret, you will hear a clash between it and the ringing open string.

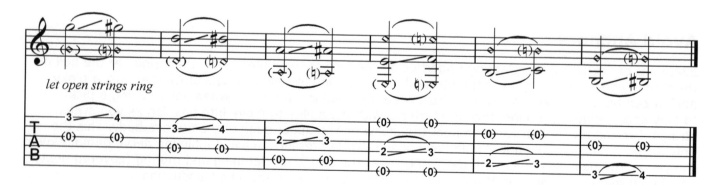

14

It's not easy to palm-damp the string immediately neighboring the one you are playing. You might accidentally damp your intended note and get no sound at all. Instead damp the lower neighboring string with the fretting hand as described in Unit 2. In this exercise the ringing string is two strings away; with practice, it's a safe distance for palm damping.

Repeat the notes and slides, this time with the heel of your palm touching the open string two strings below the note you are playing. You only need to lightly touch this string and any lower ones enough to prevent spontaneous induced vibration. If you were to pick the palm-damped string, a muted note would sound.

Track 10 continued

Don't look at your hand while you practice this. It's a feeling you want to remember and internalize.

The Crab Exercise

The next exercise is a common warmup but now we'll also use it to coordinate damping technique between the two hands. You will play four notes on each string, and only move a finger when it is absolutely necessary. Your fretting hand will look like a crab crawling on the beach in slow motion. Only one finger moves at a time.

The first note is played with the index finger. This finger then relaxes its pressure but **stays down** as you play the next note with your second finger, and so on. After four notes, only one finger moves to the next string. The other (relaxed!) three stay down on the previous string to damp that string. Each of these fingers in turn only moves over to the next string when it is needed.

Your fret-hand fingers should damp all strings higher in pitch than the one you are playing. Additionally, the upper edges of fingertips 1, 2, or 3 should damp the immediately lower neighboring string.

As in the previous exercise, the picking hand will damp starting two strings below the one you are playing. If you are playing string 4, it will damp string 6. If you are playing string 3, it will damp 5 and 6, and so on.

When you reach the top note and start to descend, you'll be removing fingers to make way for lower notes. These fingers do not just jump out of the way, however. Move them into position where they'll soon be needed, damping the next string until it is time to press it just the right amount for a good tone.

When you need to move a finger, carefully lift it off the string so that you do not accidentally pluck it or a neighboring one with your fingertip. As you finish using a string, damp it with the edges of the other fingers so it does not ring when you let it go. The object of the exercise is controlled movement to make the cleanest sounds possible. The speed is irrelevant, though there is a tendency to press down too hard when doing it very slowly.

15

Track 11 The Crab

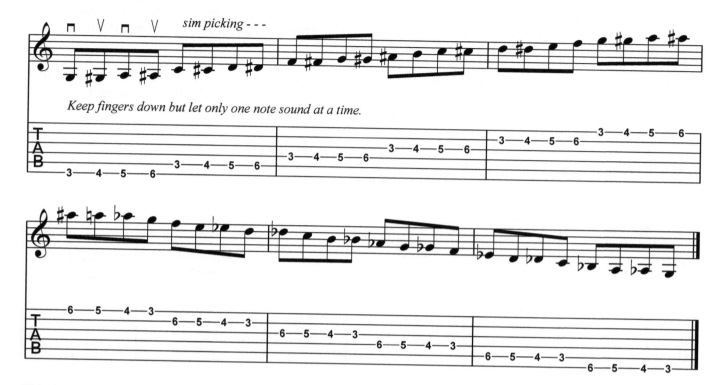

Keep fingers down but let only one note sound at a time.

This is not exactly how you will play in the long run, especially at high tempos, but you should make an effort to apply what you learn while working on it to the rest of your playing. The more you practice this way, the more professional and smooth you will sound overall. Don't let the fingers fly out or curl under the neck between notes. Keep them down on the strings whenever you can. Listen closely as you go from one note to another, and allow only the note you want to sound.

Track 12 Palm-Muted Picking

For this exercise you'll fret a note, then pick it five times. The first four times, palm-mute your alternate-picked attack so the notes are short. Slightly raise your palm off the string for the last attack so the note rings. Repeat on all six strings at various places on the fretboard.

A benefit of forearm rotation is that it helps you hit only one string at a time. When combined with palm-muting, it naturally arcs the pick away from the guitar after each upstroke. If the next note after a downstroke is on the same string, it can help you stay relaxed to let the pick or your index fingernail come to rest against the neighboring string before changing direction to play an upstroke.

The movements of picking, switching strings, and damping and muting complicate pick-hand mechanics so much that the apparently precise instructions given in this unit can only be general guidelines. The reality is that you play mostly by feel and by sound. Stay relaxed, avoid rigid anchors, and practice alternate picking in steady time with a metronome on a daily basis. Listen for the clear tone you want and let good habits form over time.

Unit 8: Synchronization

For melodic playing with clean connected tones, the pick should usually strike the string at the same time as the fretting finger. That may sound obvious, but sometimes you can find yourself blaming one hand for a flam when the other is at fault.

Let's assume for the moment you can lock in with the metronome and sound good most of the time, but a certain passage doesn't feel strong even though you're hitting all the notes. If the pick is early or the fingering late, the tone may be buzzy or choked. If the pick is late or the fretting finger early, the attacks may sound weaker by raising the general level of noise from your guitar.

To identify problems for any musical passage and help fix them you can practice each hand's timing separately, making sure that neither is rushing at slow tempos or dragging at higher ones. Both hands need to be able to do their respective jobs in time with the metronome without the other. Try keeping the practice tempo for both hands below the maximum accurate speed for either hand by itself.

Track 13 Isolate Hands, Single String

Use various metronome settings from very slow to as fast as you can play either hand without mistakes while staying relaxed.

1. Pick the damped string without fretting. Keep down- and upstrokes evenly timed.
2. Fret silently without picking. Keep your touch light, gently tapping each note. Pulloffs are not necessary here. Make sure every finger locks into the tempo.
3. Play normally with both hands while listening for solid execution.

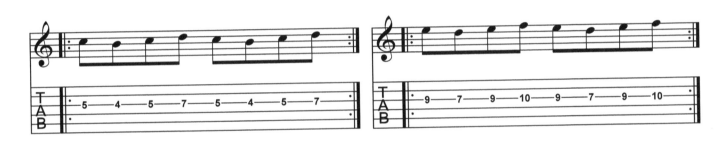

Assignment: Isolate Hands, Multiple Strings

Apply isolation of the hands to previous examples where 8th notes cross two strings or more: Tracks 4, 5, 6, 7, 9.

Unit 9: Major Scales

In any complete major scale **fingering pattern**, the lowest note is usually not the root of the **scale**. The complete fingering pattern includes all notes of the scale that you can reach without shifting your hand from that area. In Pattern 1, the lowest available *scale degree* is the 3rd; the highest scale degree is the 5th.

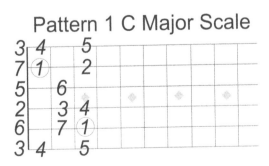

Pattern 1 C Major Scale

When learning a scale, start on a root, play all the available notes in the position, then finish on a root to drill its location into your brain. Each degree (1-7) occurs more than once, so you are repeating the scale in different octave ranges.

Pattern 1
C Major Triad

x   5   x   x

Learning the degree numbers in scale patterns is just as important as learning the names of the notes on the fretboard. Scale degree numbers are used to analyze chords and chord progressions. For example, in a three-note C major chord (a *triad*) there are a root (C), a 3rd (E), and a 5th (G). Mentally turn this vertical frame (usually used for chords) on its left side and compare to the one on the previous page. An X over a string means it is not played.

Track 14 Slow Clean Major Scale

Once you are familiar with the locations of the notes, pick the scale pattern on the previous page in time with the metronome set at a comfortable slow tempo (approximately 50-60 bpm; only adjust higher if you can play cleanly with no mistakes). Tap the toe end of your foot on the floor along with the click and name the scale degrees aloud (1-7) as you play. Practice for two minutes only. Write down your initial and final tempo for the day.

Major Scale Formula and Fretboard Patterns

The formula for a scale is created by the locations of the *half steps* (one fret apart when played on the same string) and *whole steps* (two frets apart when played on the same string).

The formula for the major scale is half steps from 3-4 and 7-8 (8 has the same pitch name as 1 but is an *octave* higher). There are whole steps between all the other pitches.

$$1\ 2\ 3\char`^4\ 5\ 6\ 7\char`^8$$

The other way to learn it is to quote the series of whole and half steps.

Whole-Whole-half-Whole-Whole-Whole-half

If you forget any scale's fingering pattern on the fretboard, you can derive it on your own using its scale formula.

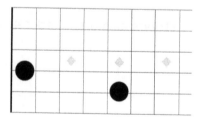

When switching strings, a **half step** is usually a distance of four frets.

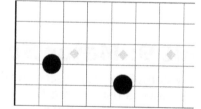

Notes a **whole step** apart are three frets away from each other on adjacent strings.

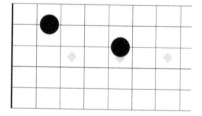

Because the tuning interval between strings 3 and 2 is different from all other string pairs, half steps and whole steps look different on that string pair. A **half step** from a note on string 3 to one on string 2 is a distance of three frets.

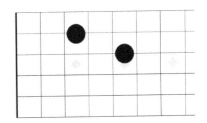

A **whole step** between strings 3 and 2 is a distance of two frets.

Half steps and whole steps underlie all other constructions, so practice to make sure you can play them on one string, or between any two adjacent strings. Include open-string notes. Don't worry about the names of the notes yet.

Unit 10: CAGED System

The major scale patterns have all their half steps (3-4 and 7-8) on one string. This helps you minimize stretches and position shifts while you are playing so it's harder to miss a note.

Pattern 2 C Major Scale

Here is Pattern 2 of the C major scale. We'll be moving our scale patterns into all twelve keys, but for now we're keeping the note C as our root to make it easier see how the five major scale patterns connect to cover the entire fretboard. For this pattern we move up to playing the 5th-string root with the middle finger.

Take your time to visualize Pattern 2, then play it without looking at the diagram. The roots are on strings 5 and 3, two frets apart. In this pattern, remember to shift the hand position by one fret when crossing between the 3rd and 2nd strings in either direction.

Pattern 1 from the previous unit is the first shape (C) of the CAGED sequence, which we can use to find anything we want on the entire fretboard. When played in open position, Pattern 1 gave us the C major scale, the reference for learning chord and scale construction (and other theory) that is common to all instruments.

Why Are These Patterns 1 & 2?

The CAGED-based 5-pattern system has gradually become the most widely-used since its introduction in the 1960s, but some teaching methods still use different pattern labeling schemes. If, for example, the previous fingering is called Pattern 4 in the system you learned, that's okay as long as your patterns are numbered consecutively and there are no gaps between patterns on the fretboard.

C, A, G, E, and D are the five open-position major chords that when connected end-to-end show the five possible shapes for any chord. Following are the CAGED system major chord shapes (*major* is implied when the quality is left off the chord name).

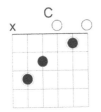
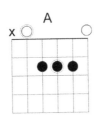
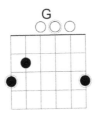
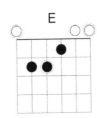
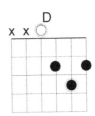

Each of the five shapes produces a C chord when it is played in the proper position to place C notes as its roots. Don't try to hold down all six strings of the following shapes; some are impossible fingerings and rarely if ever appropriate musically. Usually only parts of them are played at one time.

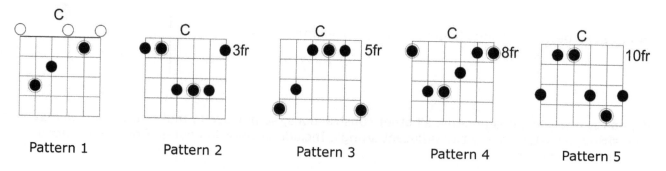

Pattern 1   Pattern 2   Pattern 3   Pattern 4   Pattern 5

Some of the *root shapes* (they are 1- and 2-octave intervals) in these patterns are also difficult stretches when played outside of open position, so they do not have to be fingered; you just need to know where the roots of a scale or chord are in relation to one another in each pattern.

Root Shapes in C

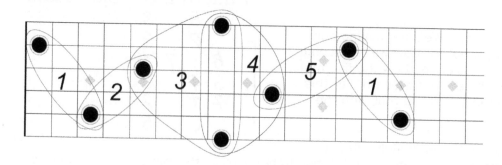

In addition to knowing the scale degree numbers, you'll need to learn the names of the notes on the guitar fretboard so you can understand theory and how melodies fit with chords. Knowing note names is also essential for communication. Make it your goal to learn the location of one note all over the fretboard per week. The five patterns of root shapes in C are a good place to start.

Root Shapes Exercise

Practice visualizing the root shapes and reciting the locations of the C notes aloud:

1st fret/2nd string	3rd fret/5th string
5th fret/3rd string	8th fret/1st string
8th fret/6th string	10th fret/4th string
13th fret/2nd string	15th fret/5th string
17th fret/3rd string	20th fret/1st string
20th fret/6th string	

After visualizing and reciting, play the C notes to confirm.

Moving the CAGED Sequence

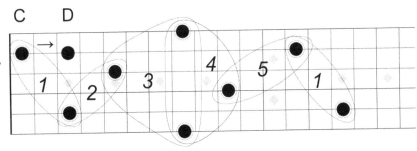

There is a D note a whole step above each C. Only one of them is shown here.

The same five root shapes apply to every D note on the fretboard. The overall CAGED pattern is the same, just two frets higher. The open D string starts a new instance of **Pattern 5**.

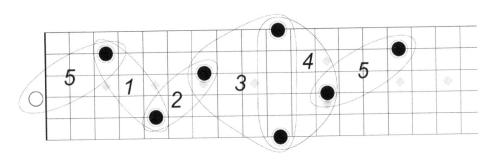

The CAGED system can be used to identify all scale patterns, chord voicings, and melodic shapes.

The open C chord shape gives us a D when played at the 2nd fret. The fingering must change; the first finger now barres the two notes that were open strings in the open-position C chord.

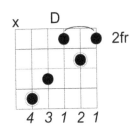

Rather than call this chord a "D major chord of the C shape" we'll hereafter refer to everything associated with this root shape as Pattern 1, making this a **Pattern 1 D major chord**. We're still using the CAGED system, but with numbers instead of letters (CAGED=12345), which will simplify the search for the right note or chord in the future.

Track 15 Pattern 1 Major Scale Without Open Strings

As with the chord, when played away from open position where we first learned it, the Pattern 1 major scale is the same shape but uses a different fingering. Now all four fingers are required.

Just as before, take your time and carefully examine the diagram and visualize how you will play it **before** you start. Mentally mark both roots and the half steps between steps 3-4 and 7-1 in each place they occur. Start playing from a root, then go all the way up and down, naming each scale degree aloud. Finish on a root.

Pattern 1 D Major Scale

Unit 11: Understanding Intervals

You don't have to fully understand this unit before practicing interval studies, but eventually you'll use its information in analysis, reading, improvising solos, and thinking about your own compositions. Re-read it after some time spent working through later ones. This is not a theory book, so we'll just cover enough to understand what we'll be playing.

An *interval* is the difference between one pitch and another, measured in terms of music rather than physics. All scales and chords are defined by the intervals between their notes. An interval name has two parts. The *quantity* is a number, usually from 1 to 13 (though there is actually no upper limit). The quantity gives a rough measurement of the interval, indicating how many steps it is up or down a scale or the musical staff. An exact measurement also includes the interval's *quality*, a word like *perfect*, *major*, or *minor*. Notes that have the same name and staff location (and are the same pitch, vibrating at the same physical frequency) are at an interval of "one" or *perfect unison*.

The yardstick of intervallic measurement is the major scale, which has seven uniquely-named notes. The eighth note starts the scale over and has the same letter name as the first, an *octave* higher. Notes an octave apart are even multiples of each other in vibratory frequency. For example, your open low E string cycles approximately 82.4 times per second. An E an octave higher—which you could play on the same string at fret 12—vibrates at about 164.8 cycles. The next higher E, two octaves above the first, is ~329.6, and so on.

Intervals are divided into two main types: **perfect** or **major**.

The **perfect** intervals are **unison (1)**, **4th**, **5th**, and **octave (8)**. Please memorize them: 1, 4, 5 8.

The **major** intervals are the **2nd**, **3rd**, **6th**, and **7th**. Memorize that list also: 2, 3, 6, 7.

The major scale is the only seven-note scale whose notes are all either a perfect or major interval from its starting note (the *root*), one reason we use it as the reference for describing anything that contains pitches: scales, chords, etc.

Compound intervals are those larger than an octave. For our purposes they are equivalent to intervals within a single octave. For example, a 2nd plus an octave is a 9th. You can subtract 7 from any compound interval to find its equivalent *simple* interval.

When a major interval is reduced in size (by lowering the upper note or by **raising the lower one**) by a half step, its quality becomes *minor*. Thus you may have a minor 2nd, 3rd, 6th, or 7th. When the now-minor interval is further reduced in size by another half step, it becomes *diminished* in quality.

A perfect interval goes straight to being a diminished interval when reduced in size. There is no minor 4th, 5th or octave.

When either main type, perfect or major, is **increased** in size by a half step, it becomes an *augmented* interval. Though you may not need to refer to all of these often, there may be an augmented 2nd, 3rd, 4th, 5th, 6th, 7th, octave, etc.

Interval Types and Changes Exercise

A. Look away from the book and recite the interval types:

perfect (1 4 5 8)

major (2 3 6 7)

B. Recite how each interval type's name changes when it is reduced or increased in size.

Augmented
MAJOR
  minor
   diminished

Augmented
PERFECT
  diminished

Enharmonics

Many intervals are *enharmonic equivalents*, with the same absolute pitches in our tempered tuning system. They sound the same but are named differently depending on the context. For example, an augmented 2nd is enharmonic to a minor 3rd. Both these intervals are a distance of three frets on a string of the guitar.

There is also enharmonic letter naming of pitches. For example, an E note may need to be named F-flat (F♭) when spelling out certain intervals, scales, or chords. For the exercises we'll be practicing, you won't need to derive these enharmonic note names yourself, but they are used correctly where they come up in the book. The letters follow the interval numbers, so a minor 3rd higher than D♭ is F♭, not its enharmonic E natural. A good rule of thumb is that each letter or number should only be used once, as when starting this D♭ major scale.

1 2 3
D♭ E♭ F♭ <-- this is not E, because E has already been used.

Diatonic Intervals

Diatonic is an important term to know. The word comes from the Greek dia- (*across*, as in *diameter* or *diaphragm*) and tonos (*tone*), and describes a span of tones: a scale. A practical definition of diatonic is "using only notes from one scale."

As long as you play notes or chords from within one scale, you are playing diatonically. Notes outside a particular scale are said to be *non-diatonic* to it.

A diatonic interval occurs between any two notes of a single scale. From each step in the major scale to the next is the interval of a diatonic 2nd. The whole steps are major 2nds, and the half steps are minor 2nds. When measuring from the root to the other notes, we have a major 2nd, major 3rd, perfect 4th, perfect 5th, major 6th, and major 7th. It's a good idea to recite, or even better sing, the numbers aloud as you play the major scale.

Define the new terms from this unit aloud.

- interval quantity, interval quality

- compound interval, simple interval

- enharmonic

- diatonic

Unit 12: Scale Skips

Diatonic interval studies will help you learn the exact distance from any note in a scale to any other. For example, from the 2nd to the 4th in the major scale is a diatonic minor 3rd.

Track 16 Diatonic 3rds in D Major Pattern 1

This is a two-note sequence: 3rds, also called **skips**, moving up one step at a time. The melodic pattern is 1-3, 2-4, 3-5 etc., on the way up, then 8-6, 7-5, 6-4, etc, on the way down. Even if you don't read music, notice how it looks on the staff. Each group of two notes (the 3rds) stays on spaces or on lines.

To help learn the sequence, try:

The RIPPS Method for Memorization

RIPPS is an acronym for a strategy to efficiently learn new material with minimum aggravation. Concentrate on one step at a time without worrying about the others. If you get stuck, move back a step.

Review, Input, Plan, Play, Stop!

Review background information. Here it's the root shape and scale pattern you will use, and a chord using notes from the same pattern. For a major scale, play the closest major chord.

Input raw data to your brain. Find the exact notes of the sequence without worrying about rhythm, fret-hand fingering, or picking accuracy. Go as slowly as necessary to make a clear mental image. Visualize the sequence without touching the guitar.

Plan. Crawl through the sequence without the metronome, addressing fingering or other technical problems as you go from note to note. This example above uses just one finger per fret, but we'll need to damp the open strings as we finish with them. Don't stress if while working on technique you sometimes forget which note is next.

Play it with the metronome at a slow tempo, using alternate-picking and an even *beat division* (usually two notes per click). Tap your foot in steady time. It's OK if you miss a note here and there while playing with the metronome. Only back up if you're making the same mistakes again and again.

Stop after playing twice through the exercise with the metronome, even though there may be mistakes. It is not supposed to be perfect the first day. Move on to something else. You'll come back to it every day for at least two weeks.

Practice the new sequence (from memory if possible) for a short time each day, adjusting your metronome up or down to a tempo where you are challenged but not frustrated. Listen for solid execution.

Track 17 3rds in C Major Pattern 2

This time the exercise is longer to cover all the available notes in Pattern 2. Make sure your foot taps evenly with the metronome as you play two notes per tap/click, except for the quarter notes (marked) which last from one foot tap until the next. Repeat signs tell you to play it a second time.

> Imperfect execution is okay while you're learning, because it is temporary. Imperfect knowledge of what you're trying to do is not, because it is permanent unless you fix it!

Track 18 Diatonic 4ths in D major Pattern 1

Try both classical fingering and rolling technique. In the end you may decide that a mixture of the two gets the cleanest sound. Please be sure you're still strictly alternate picking.

Linear Learning, Parallel Practice

If a new item seems too hard, it could mean you're trying to learn more than one thing at a time. You may be missing a prerequisite. Music is a linear subject: new pieces often depend on previous material. You'll often need to back up for review or clarification.

On the other hand, to progress at a decent pace you must alternate between concepts and let them develop in parallel. Work on one thing at a time, but don't expect the one thing you're working on **now** to be perfect before you work on something else. Without this approach, your improvement will be very slow.

Unit 13: Natural Minor

The 6th degree of any major scale is the root of a *natural minor* scale using the same pitches. The two scales are *relative*. A minor is the **relative minor** of C.

C Major

```
      ^           ^
C D E F G A B C
1 2 3 4 5 6 7 8
```

A Minor

```
    ^       ^
A B C D E F G A
1 2 3 4 5 6 7 8
```

Conversely, C major is the **relative major** of A minor. The 3rd degree of a minor scale is the root of its relative major.

```
        ^
A B C
1 2 3
```

Marking the root of a minor scale as step 6 and counting up **or** down to find the 1 gives us its relative major. This method will later be used for finding modes, so check it out!

```
    ^       ^
A B C D E F G A
6 7 1 2 3 4 5 6
→               ←
```

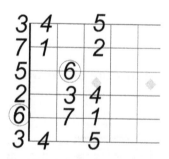

The notes on step 6 in a Pattern 1 major scale form a Pattern 2 octave shape. They are the roots of an A minor scale, sharing the fingering pattern with C major Pattern 1.

When you hear the term "minor scale" you can assume that this, the natural minor scale, is the one intended, though there are actually many minor scales (natural, harmonic, melodic, etc.).

The major scale and its relative minor also have modal names: *Ionian* and *Aeolian*, respectively.

The natural minor scale has half steps from 2-3 and 5-6. When measuring from its root to the other notes, the natural minor scale has a major 2nd, a minor 3rd, a perfect 4th and 5th, and a minor 6th and 7th. We can abbreviate the interval qualities (M for Major, m for minor, and P for Perfect) and spell the scale like this.

Natural Minor

1	M2	m3	P4	P5	m6	m7	P8

You've already played the fingering for this scale, but it may seem new when you change the numbers you recite as you play it and hear a different note as the root. In this diagram and some later ones, an *accidental* marks the notes that are not a perfect or major interval away from the root. Here the flat symbol (♭) marks the minor 3rd, 6th, and 7th of the scale. The word "flat" is used as shorthand for minor and diminished intervals, so you can say either "flat 3rd" or "minor 3rd," etc.

Pattern 2 A Minor

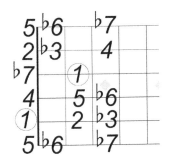

Start from the open A root, play up and down all the available notes, then finish on the root. Recite scale degrees as you play.

The perceived *tonic* (root) of a scale pattern is implied by the chord(s) it is played over and supported by the notes you choose on various beats in the music. A melodic line that places the root of either scale on beat 1 or beat 3 of a 4/4 measure will imply that it is the tonic note.

Track 19 A minor vs C Major

This distinction is so important that the two scales should be practiced separately as if they had no relationship, even though they share the same notes.

The Pattern 2 C major scale has the same notes and fingering as **Pattern 3** of A minor. The roots in any Pattern 3 scale are on strings 6, 3, and 1, three frets apart. Play this one with the metronome while reciting the new degree names.

Pattern 3 A Minor Scale

Major and Minor Chord Progressions

Another crucial part of creating a major or minor sound is the selection and order of chords, whether the chord movements are actually played or only implied by a melody or bass part.

C major:
```
1.  |C       |Am     |F    G |C    G |
        I        vi      IV   V   I    V
```

A minor:
```
2.  |Am      |G      |F      G  |Am  C  |
        i        ♭VII    ♭VI    ♭VII  i   ♭III
```

Both progressions above use the same four chords. The first has a C *tonality* (the feeling that one note is the tonic or *key center*), and a major *modality* (the effect created by the other notes around the tonic). The second progression has an A tonality, and a **minor** modality. The tonality and modality together are commonly called the *key*. The first progression is in the key of C major. The second: A minor.

Each of the progressions is diatonic: its chords contain only notes from one scale, with no key changes.

When analyzing progressions, each chord is labeled with a Roman numeral that tells which scale degree is its root. These *chord functions* show the relationship of the chords to the overall key center. For example, G is the V ("five") in the key of C major. It's common to label any chord containing a major 3rd with upper case, and any chord with a minor 3rd, lower-case. You may encounter other variations; for example some teachers label chords in minor keys without the ♭ mark on III, VI, and VII, since it is implied if the key is stated in advance.

The diatonic chords in the key of C major are:

I	C
ii	Dm
iii	Em
IV	F
V	G
vi	Am
vii	Bdim

The diatonic chords in A minor are the same, only starting from Am.

i	Am
ii	Bdim
♭III	C
iv	Dm
v	Em
♭VI	F
♭VII	G

Scalar Improvisation Exercise

Record yourself playing the chord progressions given on the previous page, eight times through each. Keep it simple but play steady time with the metronome to create your own backing track. At 72 bpm your two tracks will be about 2 minutes each.

Play the tracks back and pick single notes over them. Use all the scale tones but try to reinforce the tonality, especially by hitting the tonic note on the downbeat of measure 4. Stay in time, using only eighth notes or longer. Use lots of long notes and/or rests where you don't play anything. During these, keep listening to the chords and tapping your foot. Don't expect a brilliant solo just yet.

Even though the C major and A minor scales and keys are related and share the same notes, chord progressions will dictate that the notes be used differently for each. To solo with A minor in mind every time you have a C major-key progression can sound too random instead of like something that fits the chords.

Unit 14: Pentatonic Sequences

Most examples in the book are short and designed to resolve onto a beat, within a two, four, or eight-measure phrase. Each might end in a slightly different way. It's not necessary to memorize each one exactly as shown. Just realize that keeping track of the downbeat is one of the most important goals of practice.

You can make interval studies longer to include more notes within the reach of a position, multiple positions, or even the entire fretboard, to help you learn your way around. When improvising or composing, however, use **shorter** fragments—sometimes just one or two melodic intervals—and then develop them with repetition and variation to fit a song's phrases.

Major Pentatonic Pattern 1

The major pentatonic scale is the same as major but with degrees 4 and 7 removed. This frame does not specify the starting fret. For the key of D, put the roots on frets 5 and 3.

Track 20 Pentatonic Skips

Some pentatonic skips are 4th intervals instead of 3rds.

Major Pentatonic Pattern 2

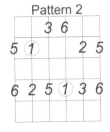

Track 21 Skips in Major Pentatonic Pattern 2

Start from the C root with your 2nd finger. Use the 3rd and 4th finger or the rolling technique with the 3rd finger on top of the 4th for the 5th-fret notes.

29

Track 22 Groups of Three, B minor Pentatonic Pattern 2

Eighth-note triplets have three evenly-spaced notes per beat, so only the first note of each will correspond exactly with a position of your tapping foot. With alternate picking, every other triplet starts with an upstroke.

Track 23

If we play the same 3-note sequence with 8th notes—two notes per beat—it creates a slightly syncopated feel. Every other group's starting note is off the beat. Take your time and work up the independence needed to keep your foot tapping with the metronome. Don't let the foot follow the hands.

Unit 15: Productive Practice Time

Practice is best done when your brain is rested. The amount of new information you can retain from a single sitting is limited. Memory from the middle of a long session is liable to be murky, so it's better to break learning into many short sessions.

When learning new material, concentrate on only one thing at a time in short focused bursts. Go very slowly, visualize what you're about to do, then play a small piece (even just 2 or 3 notes at a time) of the new pattern or lick perfectly just once. Try to make a clear impression with only one correct version in your mind. Once you know it well you can start working on variations and making new music from it, but for now, separate this experience by taking your hands off your guitar and focusing your attention somewhere else, even if it's just for a few seconds.

It is possible to work for longer stretches of time when taking music you already know up to higher tempos with the metronome, incorporating licks into your vocabulary, or composing, but try to think of practice time as **learning time**. Repetitive practice has its place, but it should not be mindless; only continuing while you're able to pay attention.

Some people recommend practicing scales while watching television. That may be better than nothing, but practice time is most productive when it is deliberate, with **no distractions**.

A much-cited 1993 study by Anders Ericsson of Florida State University found that the top-ranked of a group of violinists practiced intensely for at least 20 hours per week, but no more than four hours per day total. Several 90-minute or shorter sessions worked best, separated by time for recovery. The better players also slept more hours per week and took more naps than the weaker ones. This study and similar ones tell us much about the most efficient ways to learn.

Schedule your first session as early as possible in the day. Plan sessions of no more than 90 minutes, starting and ending at specific times. This is especially important if the time must be different on some days. Suppose you're not naturally an early riser but have a part-time job from 9:00 am to 1:00 PM four days per week. On your days off, start your first practice at 9—because it's already your habit to be active then. Now here's the important part: also set an exact time to start and stop on the workdays. Not just "after work whenever I feel ready," but for example 2:30-3:30.

Specific planning of a routine that avoids the use of will power or daily decision-making is the only way to create a practice habit. If you tend to put off or feel subconscious resistance to starting, try spending the end of one session precisely defining what you're going to do in the next one. When you know what exactly what to do and when to do it, it is easier to start.

Track 24 Diatonic 4ths in Pattern 2

The fingering shown is only one of several viable approaches. Stay with alternate picking for steady rhythm.

Major Scale Pattern 3

To get Pattern 3 in the key of C, for example, you'd play the C roots on frets 8, 5, and 8. This pattern is also equivalent to A minor, Pattern 4, with roots on frets 5, 7, and 5.

Familiarize yourself with this new pattern by **R**eviewing the root shape, **I**nputting the fretboard locations visually, **P**lanning your fingering, **P**laying it slowly without looking at the diagram, and then **S**top.

Interval Study Assignment

Now that you've seen diatonic 3rds and 4ths in a couple of patterns, it's time to start working interval studies out by yourself. Take your time and figure out 3rds and 4ths throughout Pattern 3 of the major scale. If you're up to the challenge, find starting and stopping beats and modify the exercises to break them into phrases. It's OK to repeat a note, start on an offbeat, or use other rhythmic variations to resolve onto a strong beat.

Unit 16: The Rock Box

Pattern 3 C Major Pentatonic

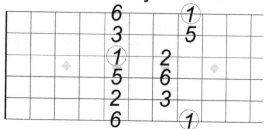

Here's C major pentatonic Pattern 3, created by omitting degrees 4 and 7 of the major scale.

Track 25 Major Pentatonic Groups of Three

For triplets, you'll play three evenly-spaced notes per tap of the foot. When you alternate-pick this example you will have an upstroke on every other downbeat.

Pattern 4 A Minor Pentatonic

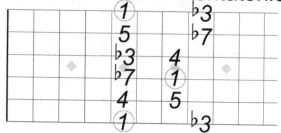

The same fingering is equal to Pattern 4 minor pentatonic. Now the omitted scale degrees are 2 and 6.

If by now you are playing with the metronome and tapping your foot without too much difficulty, then it's time to start counting beats aloud as you play. This is an important ability to develop but it can be difficult because it requires you to do three things at once: count, tap, and play. Since it's likely you already know Pattern 4 of minor pentatonic, it's a good place to start counting beats as you play.

As usual, start by practicing the scale in eighth notes: two evenly-spaced notes per click. Your toe hits the floor along with the click and reaches its highest point exactly halfway before the next click.

Track 26 Pentatonic Skips in Triplets

The syncopation can make this example hard to figure out, so practice in two-beat chunks. It's also a good idea to write it out from memory on your own.

Economy Picking

Alternate picking where possible is best for good feel and timing. Master it first and make it the default. Only switch to a different method when you have a good reason. Economy picking can make some sequences easier to play fast and clean, and along with legato technique can make for a looser feel.

Track 27 Economy Downstrokes

Strike a fretted note on the 3rd string with a downstroke and let the pick follow through and come to rest against the 2nd string until it is time for the next note. It's not a chord strum. Lift the fingertips just enough between notes to make sure they stay separated.

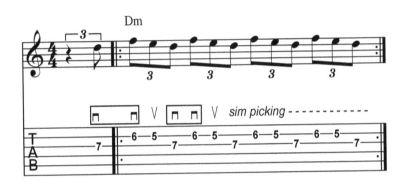

Economy picking should eventually let you play some things faster, but make sure you keep an even tempo and don't rush the consecutive downstrokes. Work up the metronome setting very gradually.

Track 28 Descending Pentatonic Groups of 5

Only the groups that start with the 3rd or 4th finger of the fretting hand are used here. The result is a repeated down-up-down-up-down picking pattern. Although the notation appears to say you're starting the next group with the same downstroke, you want a rhythmically separated rest stroke.

By adding up to eight these fit easily into even time feels. Again, playing only the groups that start with the 3rd or 4th finger lets you use an economy picking pattern.

Unit 17: Legato and String Skipping

As a general musical term *legato* means *connected*. One note sustains until the next one starts, but with no overlap. On the guitar, this often means that after the first note on a given string is picked, one or more subsequent ones are played with hammer-ons or pull-offs, lessening the percussive aspect of the note attack.

The separation between successive notes is called *articulation*. To cleanly articulate hammer-ons and pull-offs at sufficient volume and with rhythmic accuracy, your fingers may have to come off the strings a little higher than for picked notes. Keep your fingers arched when executing hammer-ons so that you only hit the target string.

Likewise, avoid bumping into the neighboring strings when pulling off to a lower note. The little snap of the fingertip required to set the string into motion means you can't keep the 2nd, 3rd, and 4th fingers down as much as when picking the normal way. When pulling off to the 1st finger or an open string, avoid letting your forearm rotate so that the fingers flail out. Pull-offs and hammer-ons require energetic execution but should not push or pull the string out of tune.

To make sure you don't rush the unpicked notes, practice in strict time with the metronome, working on each hand separately if needed.

Track 30 Legato Crab

We can adapt the crab exercise to drill the basic legato movements.

Try it as shown, pulling off and hammering as many notes as possible, then repeat, alternating between one picked and one legato note.

Track 31 Legato 3rds

We can apply hammer-ons and pull-offs on any existing practice items that have two or more notes on any string: scales, interval studies, and pentatonic sequences.

Move the pick slightly away from the string so you do not strike it during the hammer-ons and pull-offs, but keep the pendulum-like momentum of alternate picking for steady timing. On these legato diatonic 3rds in Pattern 3 an upstroke is followed by a pull-off, so the next pick attack is another upstroke.

Legato technique can create interesting accent patterns where some notes are naturally more pronounced than others. The trade-off is that you can lose some of the percussion and groove of picked notes. Deciding when to use legato versus picking can make a lick come to life, so listen closely to determine when other players are picking versus pulling/hammering, and listen to yourself as you experiment.

String Skipping

Bigger movements of the picking hand make it harder to be accurate, so slow down your practice. Make sure nothing interferes with the picking hand's free movement, like anchoring, fanning out your fingers, or excessive tightening of the arm. Step up the string damping in the fretting hand for insurance. Concentrate on how it feels to find the right string rather than relying on just your eyes.

Track 32 Diatonic 5ths in D Major Pattern 1

Track 33 Diatonic Sixths

When we play diatonic 6ths with minimal position shifting we'll have lots of string skips. These are in the key of E major, using scale Pattern 2.

Outside Picking

Between any two strings, *outside* picking means downstrokes on the lowest-pitched string and upstrokes on the higher-pitched one. *Inside* picking is the opposite: upstrokes on the lower-pitched string and downstrokes on the higher-pitched one. With strict alternation, the direction change on the top string in the previous 6th example results in inside picking on the way down.

In outside picking, a solid pick stroke executed with forearm rotation leaves you in position for the next note at the end of its arc. Many players prefer to continue outside picking on the descending part of the above example.

Track 34 Diatonic Sixths Outside Picking

Try the previous 6ths example again, this time adding a pull-off before measure 3 to start it with an upstroke as shown here.

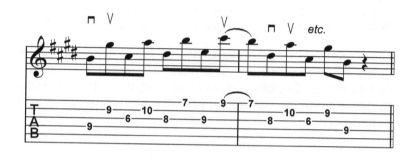

If you're looping the exercise, you could also hammer on from the last note to the first to change direction again. When a method different from alternate picking is used, the foot should keep tapping with the metronome even though your hand may be moving in the opposite direction.

Inside Picking

When inside picking, especially on two neighboring strings, the usual pick arc produced by forearm rotation has to stop early to change direction, and it can be hard to skip over the string just played. Since the distance your pick must move to reach the next string is actually shorter, you can try concentrating the picking movement into your thumb and index finger instead of using forearm rotation for these notes. It's not as powerful a stroke, but it's accurate and helps keep your wrist from tightening.

Track 35 Inside Picking Example

This excerpt from "Mojito" shows the problem and is good for practicing inside picking technique. The phrases groove best when alternate picking, with upstrokes on the offbeat pickup notes. Try just flexing the thumb joint to grab the upstroke on the lower string. Extend the thumb to hit the downbeat note.

* flex the thumb to pick marked notes.

Unit 18: Completing the Fretboard

We need to add the last couple of major scale patterns to the practice cycle, reinforcing them with more interval studies.

Pattern 4

Interval Study Assignment

Review Pattern 4 of the major scale, then work out diatonic 3rds, 4ths, 5ths, and 6ths.

Track 36 Reversed 3rds in Pattern 4

This time we're in the key of G major, which puts us in 2nd position.

Track 37 Pentatonic Double Stops

These are the same intervals (3rds and 4ths) used for pentatonic skips. Patterns 3 and 4 are a good place to play the notes simultaneously, and do some sliding to add soul. These make great fills in all styles. They're in D major here, but should eventually be practiced in every key.

Track 38 Pentatonic Double Stops, Groups of 4

This will really get these double stops under our fingers.

Major Scale Pattern 5

Pattern 5

Here's the last of the five positional fingering patterns. It's probably the hardest one to get used to and may take longer to master but it connects Pattern 4 with Pattern 1, leaving no blackout areas on the fretboard. Most melodic phrases and licks will be easier in some patterns and harder in others, so none should be neglected.

Interval Study Assignment

As with the other patterns, work out diatonic 3rds, 4ths, 5ths and 6ths in Pattern 5 and rotate them into your practice. The first few notes of each are shown here in C major. Pattern 5 will present some new fingering permutations.

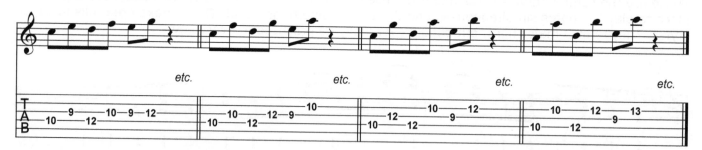

More about Practice

Everyone's mind will wander a bit, and we have to accept this while gently steering it back to the matter at hand. If your mind wanders excessively while you're playing an exercise with no mistakes, it is time to move on to one that taxes your brain more. Use the technique-building exercises in this book to warm up and to develop your hands and ears, and then also practice songs and solos that challenge you but are realistically attainable at your level. Keeping your own balance between ease and difficulty will eventually enable you to reach a state where you feel you are a mere conduit as your art seems to flow through you from a higher place. This feeling cannot be forced but comes more often as you develop your musical fluency.

When the guitar is in your hands you should always be listening; always feeling what your body is telling you; continually pursuing musical discovery as much as possible. If you don't do these things, you may miss noticing places where you can improve, you may injure yourself by overpracticing or playing with tension, or you may forget what you're ultimately trying to achieve, which is to touch the hearts and minds of your audience through self-expression. Practice with feeling to train yourself to perform with feeling.

Maintain a relaxed patient confidence as you break the work down into small bits. Your practice attitude is what you will project when you hit the stage, so don't practice cursing and tearing your hair out!

Unit 19: Modes of the Major Scale

A *mode* of a scale is one of the different ways that same series of whole and half steps can be used. Think of how a mobile phone has related but separate modes of operation (voice, text, web, etc.). We've already seen the major scale and its relative minor. Those are two of the seven major-scale modes.

We know the first mode, Ionian, is just the major scale. In the Ionian mode, there are half steps from 3-4 and 7-8. Each scale degree is either a perfect or major interval from the root (1).

Ionian

| 1 | M2 | M3 | P4 | P5 | M6 | M7 | P8 |

The sixth mode, Aeolian, is the same as the natural minor scale. Aeolian has a minor 3rd, 6th, and 7th. The half steps are from 2-3 and 5-6.

Aeolian

| 1 | M2 | m3 | P4 | P5 | m6 | m7 | P8 |

We learned that starting from step 6 of the major scale and making that note the new root gives us this minor scale, but that using it convincingly requires different phrasing and resolutions.

Theoretical vs. Direct

That's the split between two ways to think about modes. There is some overlap between the two, and both are important. In the theoretical approach we examine how modes are related to major scales and key centers and also to each other, sharing the same notes and to a great extent the same fingerings (*Chord Tone Soloing*, Ch. 12, 14, 19).

We can also think of the modes as discrete scales applicable to specific chords, learning to spell them from their own respective roots. This book makes this direct way its focus. It requires learning patterns with redundant fingerings, but allows immediate use of modes for improvisation. So, rather than playing G major when we want A Dorian because the two scales share the same notes, now we're going to learn A Dorian as if it were a completely new and different sound.

Dorian: Mode ii

Dorian has a minor 3rd and a minor 7th, but a **major 6th**. The half steps are from 2-3 and 6-7.

Dorian

| 1 | M2 | m3 | P4 | P5 | M6 | m7 | P8 |

For most players, Pattern 4 of each mode is easier than the others to find and use at first. Here is Pattern 4 of A Dorian.

Only the major 6th sets Dorian apart from Aeolian. Compare Pattern 4 of Dorian with Pattern 4 of Aeolian (page 31). Play both patterns several times, reciting the degrees aloud as you go.

Pattern 4 A Dorian

	1		2	♭3	
	5		6	♭7	
2	♭3		4		
6	♭7		1		
	4		5		
	1		2	♭3	

Track 39 Dorian Improv

Once you have the pattern under your fingers, try it over this two-chord *vamp* (a short chord progression that repeats indefinitely). You can get a sense of movement if you play the ♭7 (G) over the Am7 chord and save the distinctive 6th degree of the mode (F♯) for the D7 chord.

Compare this with the Aeolian progression on page 27 (Am - G - F, etc.).

Modal Pattern Assignment

Find the other patterns of the Dorian mode by raising the 6th degree of minor Patterns 1, 2, 3, 5.

Minor Variations

Often a melody uses the minor pentatonic scale only or does not happen to use the sixth degree. The major or minor 6th may be present in the chords, however, which would determine which mode you'd use if you were to embellish the melody or take a solo over the progression. If the 6th is nowhere to be found in the chords or any melodic part (including vocals), try to choose based on the style of the song. Dorian is often used in roots rock and blues-based styles. Aeolian is more traditionally classical-sounding and is used in all kinds of music from folk to pop and hard rock.

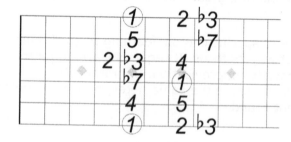

Common variations are produced by leaving some notes out of the scale. These two will fit in either Aeolian or Dorian contexts. Here's minor pentatonic with the 2nd added:

1 2 ♭3 4 5 ♭7

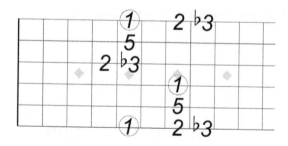

The **1 2 ♭3 5** variation is often played across more than one octave.

Minor pentatonic with a major 6th replacing the ♭7 (**1 ♭3 4 5 6**) is a colorful sound over Am7 and is also equal to a D9 arpeggio.

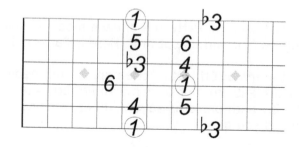

Connecting Major Patterns

With the previous inclusion of Pattern 5 we now have patterns of major scales that cover the entire fretboard. We can play all over the neck in any key. Here are the five patterns, for example, in the key of F. The lowest F note on the guitar is on fret 1 of string 6, so the system starts with root shape 4 and includes some open-string notes.

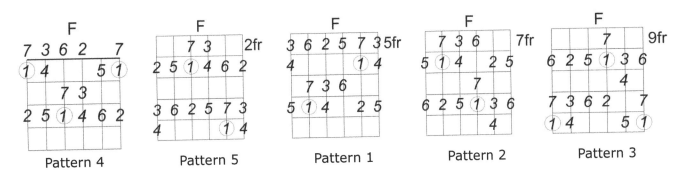

Pattern 4   Pattern 5   Pattern 1   Pattern 2   Pattern 3

Each positional scale pattern has three notes per string except for one string that has only two notes. (Pattern 2 has two notes on strings 6 & 1.) By adding one note on any string we move into the neighboring pattern. For example, here we move from Pattern 1 to Pattern 2 by stretching or sliding up on string 3.

Shifting Exercise

Slide, shift, or stretch to get an extra note on any string to move back and forth between any two patterns, visualizing one in your head while you play the other. Stay with only two patterns at a time for now.

Key Changes

When the five patterns are learned, we can also switch between any keys without moving the hand by more than one fret in either direction. This requires and reinforces knowledge of the note names on the fretboard.

Here is an A major scale passage, then one in C major in the same position. At the fourth fret, A major uses Pattern 4, while C major uses Pattern 3.

Track 40

Key-Switching Exercise

Start in any key, and pick a position on the neck. Play the major scale with the correct pattern number for that position. Then play the major scale of a new key, using the least possible amount of shifting. For example, first play C major Pattern 4 at 7th position. Then go up a fourth interval and play F major Pattern 2 in the same position. Next play Pattern 5 of B♭, and so on.

Unit 20: Mixolydian—Mode V

Mixolydian only differs from the major scale (a.k.a. the Ionian mode) by having a ♭7.

Mixolydian

| 1 | M2 | M3 | P4 | P5 | M6 | m7 | P8 |

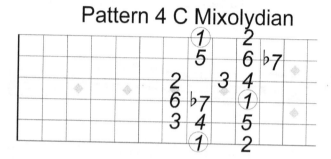

Pattern 4 C Mixolydian

For Pattern 4 of Mixolydian play the low root with your 2nd finger and shift up by one fret when you reach the 2nd string.

Modal Pattern Assignment

Find the other patterns of the Mixolydian mode by flatting the 7th degree of major scale Patterns 1, 2, 3, and 5.

Both Ionian and Mixolydian have major 3rds. If there is a tonic (I) major triad and no 7th scale degree is present in the music, then depending on the style either mode may be an option. When a 7th of the tonality is present it will dictate which of these two modes is the right one to play.

The Mixolydian mode fits a dominant 7th chord. The word *dominant* here means a major triad with a minor 7th added to create a four-note chord (1-3-5-♭7). (*Dominant* is also used to name the 5th degree of a scale.) The easiest fingering of the C7 chord in Pattern 4 is the barred version with two roots and two 5ths.

The voicing 1-♭7-3-5 eliminates the duplicated notes. Try the fingering shown as well as using your thumb and a 1st-finger barre (T-1-2-1). When playing blues or funk it can sound better to omit the low root, especially if the bass player is on that note. For jazz accompaniment you might omit the 2nd-string 5th degree also, resulting in a two-note chord containing the 7th and 3rd only.

Interval studies can be structured to fit the modes and train your phrasing instincts within them. Putting a long note on (or a rest after) downbeats helps you stay aware of the timing of those beats in 1-, 2- or 4-bar phrases. This makes a final resolution in the following descending diatonic 3rds in Pattern 4 C Mixolydian.

Track 41 3rds in Mixolydian

Here we resolve to chord tones 3/4 of the way through measures 1 and 2, then 3/4 through the bigger 4-bar phrase.

Track 41 continued

Track 42 Static Mixolydian Improvisation

Once you have the pattern under your fingers, try improvising with it over this vamp. Between these two chords all the notes of the C Mixolydian mode are included, so we can be sure it's the correct mode for the situation.

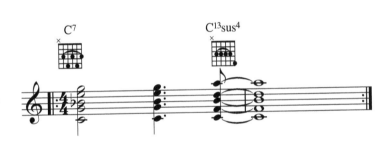

Since this C7 vamp is *static* (not progressing—in this case, especially not into the keys of F major or D minor, to which it is diatonic), we can easily add the #9 (D# or E♭ here, depending on which will minimize the use of written accidentals) for a blues inflection. Try using the #9 to slur (slide up or hammer on) to the 3rd (E) both as a *grace* note (meas. 1) and in strict time (meas. 3 and 4).

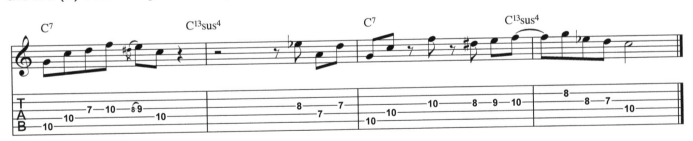

The same will apply to get a blues sound over a I7 chord that is moving to IV, as we'll see in the next section. Notice that you likely won't want to use this note on the V7 chord in a traditional diatonic progression (like a jazz standard or a pop song), because it might make the V feel like a I in a new key. You'd have better luck with it on the V in a blues.

Functioning Dominant Chords

In a diatonic major progression only the V chord has the dominant quality. By playing the major scale based on the key center you automatically get the correct notes for the corresponding Mixolydian scale for the V7 chord. No change is needed.

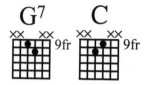

The V7 chord is said to be *functioning* because the tension of degrees 7 and 4 in the major scale encourage a resolution to the I chord, to degrees 1 and 3, respectively. We can call the I chord the *intended target* of the V. Even if the V chord is followed by a chord other than I, Mixolydian is still the right scale for it.

Secondary Dominants

Non-diatonic dominant 7th chords and major triads are very common in songs. Depending on how the non-diatonic notes in these new chords relate to the key center, one of several scales may apply. The ones in this section all take the Mixolydian mode.

The respective Mixolydian mode is used over a new dominant chord whose intended target is one of the other diatonic major triads (V or IV). These are two of the possible **secondary dominant** chords.

The V/V (five of five) is a II7 chord. In the key of C, the V/V is a D7 that replaces Dm. The intended target of D7 is G, so we temporarily switch to D Mixolydian, then return to using the C major scale for the rest of the progression.

Track 43

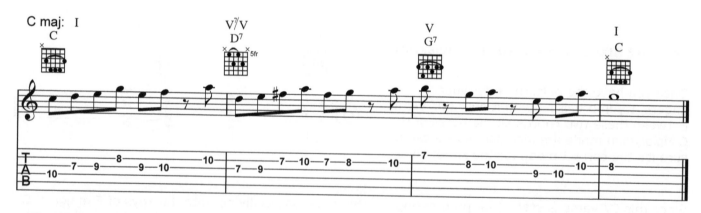

Even if the D7 is not followed by G or G7 we know that a G-major-triad-based chord is its intended target in the key of C, so we play D Mixolydian on it anyway.

Track 44

44

The other secondary dominant whose intended target is a major triad is the V/IV: the I7. In the key of G this time, a G7 replaces a G major triad or Gmaj7 chord. Often a I major triad will become dominant before it moves to the IV chord. As on Track 42, a functioning I7 is also a spot where the #9 can be used.

Track 45

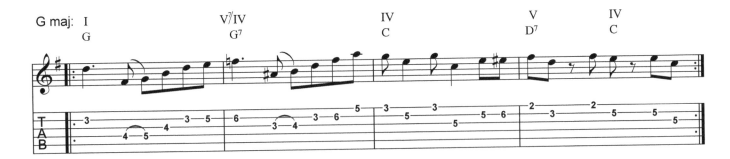

Even if it is followed by a different chord, the I7's intended target of IV major tells us to play Mixolydian.

Track 46

Mixolydian is not always the correct scale for any dominant chord. You'll find many more situations that require additional scales that are beyond our scope now. One simple way to start playing over nondiatonic chords (or alterations to diatonic chords) that usually works is to stay in the scale based on the key center and only change the note(s) needed to accommodate the new chord. In the case of the particular secondary dominants mentioned here, this produces the same notes as Mixolydian from the root of the chord.

D7 (V/V in the key of C) has the tones D-F#-A-C. The F# is the only departure from the C major scale, making it C Lydian, with the same pitches as D Mixolydian.

C D E F# G A B C

C7 (V/IV in the key of C) has the tones C-E-G-B♭. Changing the B in the C major scale to B♭ gives us C Mixolydian.

C D E F G A B♭ C

The approach works for E7 (V/vi in the key of C, a chord we haven't covered before), but does not produce Mixolydian (it produces an A *harmonic minor* scale). E7 has the tones E-G#-B-D. Changing the G in the C major scale to G# gives us the notes that work.

C D E F G#A B C

This process is quick and makes sense to the ear in context with surrounding chords, but it becomes less practical when new chords contain more than one nondiatonic note. *Chord Tone Soloing* and *Harmonic Minor, Melodic Minor and Diminished Scales* complete the vocabulary for most common harmonic situations.

Unit 21: 3rds and 6ths Across the Board

Diatonic 3rds and 6ths moving up and down the fretboard are common soloing devices that will solidify knowledge of scale and mode patterns. Start with double-stop 3rds in the D major scale on the top two strings. You'll cross through all five patterns of the D major scale. Each double stop is a partial Pattern 1 or Pattern 5 major or minor chord.

Track 47 Diatonic 3rds in D major in Double Stops

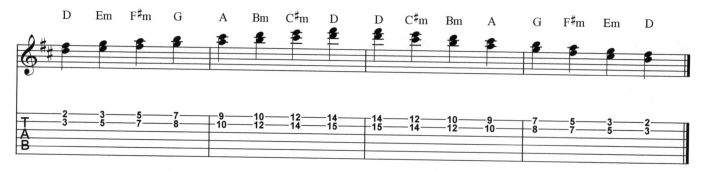

Track 48 Sliding and Ringing Double Stops

Now try the same notes picked separately but left ringing together as you slide. This gets a nice cascading sound that's good for most styles. Using the 3rd finger for all the 2nd-string notes in this example will help you keep your place.

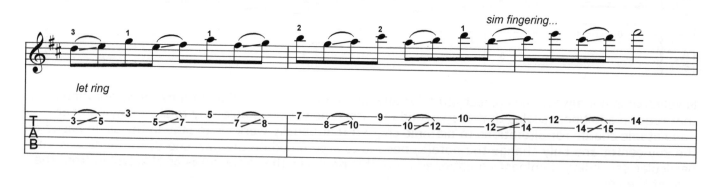

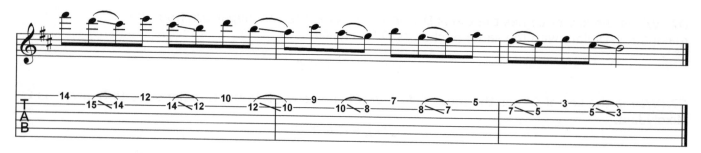

As you become familiar with the moves, name the pattern numbers in D major aloud as you go from one to the next. At any point in a series of double-stop or chord shapes up or down a stringset, you'll want to be able to stop traversing the fretboard and play positionally using the appropriate pattern. For example, if you were to stop with your index finger at ninth position, you'd be ready to play in Pattern 4.

Track 49 Switching From Horizontal (Stringset) to Vertical (Fretboard Position)

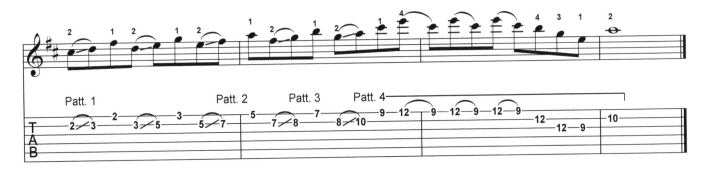

Complementary Intervals

When a 3rd is *inverted* (the lower note is raised by an octave, or the higher note is dropped by an octave) you get its *complementary* interval, a 6th. Complementary intervals add together to make an octave and are inversions of one another. The complementary simple intervals are:

2nds & 7ths	3rds & 6ths	4ths & 5ths

To play diatonic 6ths complementary to the 3rds we just heard, we can start by dropping the 1st-string F♯ to string 4, fret 3. Pluck only the 4th and 2nd strings here. If you're strumming these shapes as double-stops, damp the open 3rd string into complete silence using the underside of the finger being used to fret the lower note.

The 6ths are best identified by the chords they imply, the same as their complementary 3rds. For example, although the first 6th here (F# - D) is a minor interval, it's best to think of it as a partial D major chord that you can use for accompaniment and soloing.

Track 50 6ths in D major

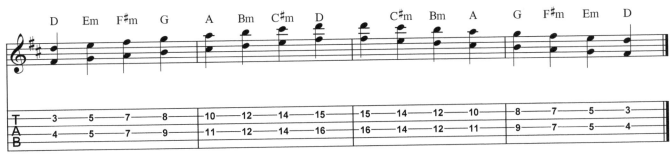

Track 51 3rds and 6ths Outlining Harmony

The two notes of each diatonic double stop are factors of a I, IV, or V chord. Using the open strings to provide the D, G, and A bass notes helps us hear the chord function. In practice, you usually would not play all these notes by yourself. Some would be implied, or picked up by another instrument, if there is one.

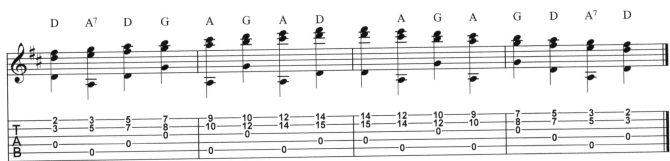

The next example has passing tones between the marked chord inversions (there's also an upper neighbor tone on the "and" of beat 3 in measure 4). These voicings would work well in a trio setting.

Track 52 6ths Practice

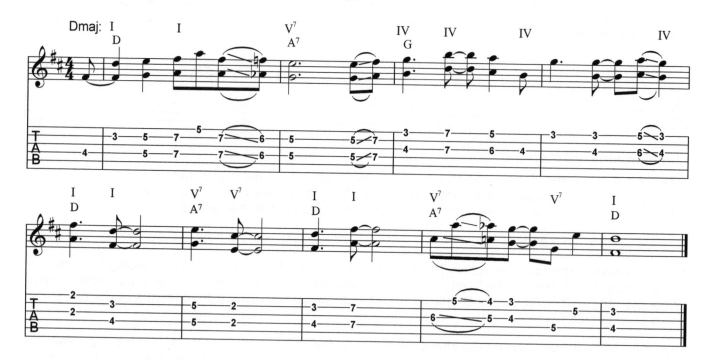

Track 53 3rds Practice

Here's the same example with the lower voice raised an octave to produce 3rds. It works the same harmonically but because this particular set of voicings is higher it might stand out better than the one above when played over another rhythm part.

Include diatonic 3rds and 6ths in your practice schedule on an ongoing basis. Make sure you can play 6ths and 3rds in any key, and across all the strings. For example, next we have 6ths in the key of B♭ using lower stringsets 5 & 3, then 4 & 2.

Track 54 Diatonic 6ths in B-flat major

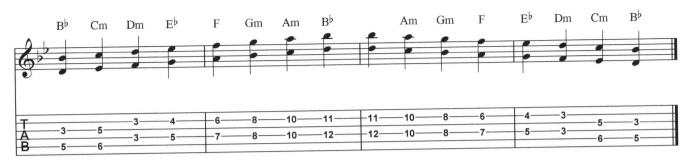

Track 55 3rds and 6ths in Minor Keys

Here we have 3rds and 6ths over a progression in A minor. If you're playing with just a drummer and bassist, you have lots of freedom to suspend chords (e.g., using an F chord over a G in the bass). If someone else is playing complete chords, listen carefully for clashes and change timing or pitch to adapt.

Track 56 Chromatic Double Stops

In each place where there are two double stops of the same quality a whole step apart in a harmonized scale or mode you can try a chromatic double stop between them. They're especially useful in Mixolydian for dominant chords in blues or country as shown here. The A and E pedal tones provide the tonal center and rhythmic breath between accents.

Apply chromatic 3rds and 6ths in Mixolydian on each stringset in the keys you are most likely to use.

Unit 22: Lydian—Mode IV

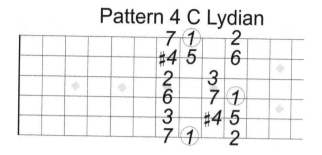

Pattern 4 C Lydian

Compare C Lydian to C major. It differs only by having a #4.

Lydian

| 1 | M2 | M3 | A4 | P5 | M6 | M7 | P8 |

Modal Pattern Assignment

Find the five patterns of the Lydian mode by raising the 4th degree of each major scale pattern.

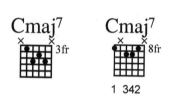

You'll choose between Lydian or Ionian over major 7 chords; Pattern 2 and Pattern 4 have easy voicings.

Theoretically, Lydian fits over the IVmaj7 chord in a major progression, over the ♭VImaj7 in a minor progression, and on any non-diatonic maj7 chord. Try Lydian on **any** maj7 chord that is neither the tonic chord of a major key nor the ♭III in a minor key.

While these guides are theoretically correct, Lydian can sound too jazzy if you use it in roots styles.

If there is a major triad or maj7 chord and no 4th scale degree is present in the immediately surrounding music, Lydian may be an option depending on the style. When a 4th of the tonality is present it will dictate which mode is the right one to play. Perfect 4th—play Ionian. Augmented 4th— play Lydian.

Here are some phrases where C Lydian is especially emphasized to help you hear it quickly. One typical static Lydian vamp starts with a major triad which then moves up by a whole step. Play the Lydian mode of the lower chord. You'll automatically get Mixolydian for the higher chord; this means you can also try these phrases over D7 by itself. The #4th of the mode (F# in this example) is the 3rd of the higher chord. Often the bass note pedals to maintain the listener's tonic orientation. The result is a *slash chord* with a name like D/C ("D over C").

Track 57

50

Fleetwood Mac's "Dreams" is an example of a static Lydian situation. All notes of the F Lydian mode eventually appear in its arrangement. If you listen to the song you'll notice that it's unnecessary or even inappropriate to emphasize the #4 in the melody. It's already present in the chords. Sometimes you just have to make sure you don't hit the perfect 4th by accident in a melodic part.

Track 58 3rds in Lydian

Some legato technique is appropriate to the Lydian sound. Here we have resolutions 3/4 of the way through a pair of 2-bar phrases structured to fit the mode and train phrasing instincts within it.

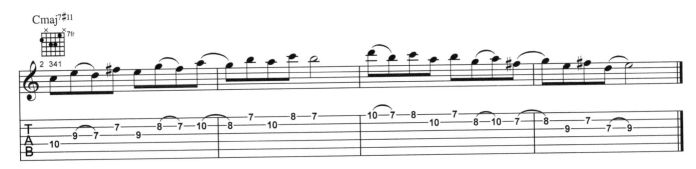

Diatonic 7ths

Practice the difficult parts of 7th interval studies in isolation, because in melodic playing you'll encounter similar challenges often. Let's review the RIPPS method while we work on these.

Review the root shape and scale for the example. This time we're using root shape 3 in 5th position. Play the C roots on strings 6, 3, and 1, play the scale mode once, then play a C major chord to reinforce the sound.

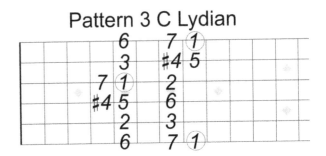

Input the locations of the notes in the sequence. That's hard enough. Don't think about how you're going to finger those notes or pick the string skips yet.

Track 59 Diatonic 7ths

Now **P**lan. If you use a finger roll on same-fret note pairs across three strings (like the one marked with a box) you'll find it is hard (but not impossible!) to avoid slapping the finger down and creating unwanted tones at higher tempos. There is an alternative fingering written that requires some planning and practice but comes out sounding pretty clean.

Play with the metronome, even if you have to do so in quarter notes (one note per click) at 50 bpm. It's not supposed to be perfect yet, so don't stress over it. After twice through the example,

Stop! Take a short break where you don't think about music, then move on to something else.

Custom Picking Directions

As well as experimenting with fret-hand fingering options, you can try different picking approaches for a given lick, then practice doing it the easiest and best-sounding way, using any combination of alternate, economy, legato, and so on. This does not mean you let your picking hand do whatever it wants. It is actually more work to do this right so that you don't paint yourself into a corner.

Track 60 Picking Direction Study

Try the familiar pentatonic triplets with alternate picking first, then check out the picking directions shown here: up, down, hammer-on, up, then economy downstrokes. Repeat starting on the next string.

The picking pattern breaks with a pull-off on the top string when the direction changes in measure 3. Then economy outside picking connects the groups of 3 and 5.

If you come up with a set of picking directions that works better for you, write it down so you can practice it the same from day to day. It's OK to change your mind as long as you are deliberate.

Unit 23: Phrygian—Mode iii

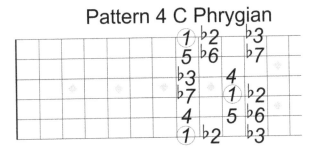

Pattern 4 C Phrygian

Compare C Phrygian Pattern 4 to C Aeolian Pattern 4. It differs only by having a ♭2.

Phrygian

1	m2	m3	P4	P5	m6	m7	P8

Modal Pattern Assignment

Find the other patterns of the Phrygian mode by flatting the 2nd degree of minor scale patterns 1, 2, 3, and 5.

Both Aeolian and Phrygian have minor 3rds and 7ths. If there is a minor triad or m7 chord and no 2nd scale degree is present in the music, depending on the style Phrygian may be an option. Phrygian will sound darker, and depending on the context, more foreign or exotic than Aeolian or Dorian. When a ♭2 of the key is present in the chords immediately surrounding a tonic minor, the Phrygian mode is the right one to play.

A typical Phrygian situation is a tonic minor chord with a major triad a half step above, or a minor triad a whole step below. The ♭2 is the root of the higher chord, and the minor 3rd of the lower. Playing Phrygian from the root of the tonic chord will give you Lydian on the higher chord and Dorian on the lower chord.

The chords in this example include all (and only) notes of C Phrygian, so we know it's the correct mode for the situation.

Track 61

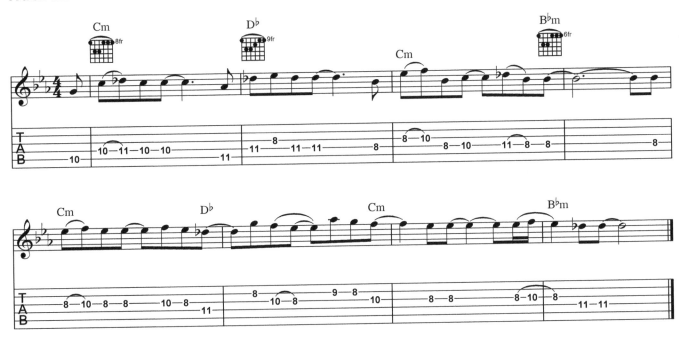

53

It can sound awkward to hit the ♭2 directly on a beat over the Im chord in steady linear playing. Try placing the ♭2 on an upbeat in your line, or save it to play over one of the neighboring chords that contain that note. You can also specifically linger on the ♭2 so that the listener can have time to accept its dissonance.

More Pattern Connection

Drilling both horizontal movement (up and down the neck) and vertical (across the strings within one pattern) will eventually eliminate blind spots in your mental picture of the fretboard.

Run the scale patterns until you can play one while visualizing its neighbor. Then when playing an interval study, add an extra interval on any stringset to move from one pattern to the next. This is preparation for sustaining melodic ideas as you change positions. The next example has alternating 4ths in E Phrygian with a shift on the 3-2 stringset between Patterns 2 and 3 and a shift on the 2-1 stringset to get to Pattern 4. The Roman numerals indicate the position of the fret-hand index finger.

Track 62

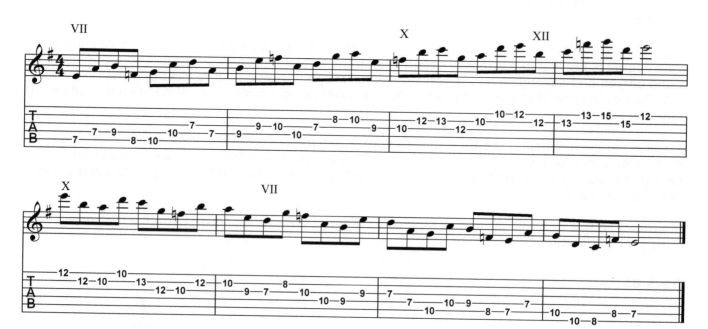

Track 63

This excerpt from "Wrecked on the Sirens' Rocks" moves between Patterns 3, 2, and 1 of A Phrygian.

54

Unit 24: Triad Arpeggios

Not every possible pattern is shown for the material in the next several units. Once you understand the basic ideas, take the initiative and work out the rest on your own. It's better that way. To remind you to explore the full landscape, there are examples from each of the five patterns.

To arpeggiate all the diatonic triads for a given key, play two consecutive diatonic 3rds from each scale degree.

Triads of the Harmonized Major Scale

Degree & Quality	Spelled from Key	Spelled from Its Own Root
I major	1-3-5	1-3-5
ii minor	2-4-6	1-♭3-5
iii minor	3-5-7	1-♭3-5
IV major	4-6-8	1-3-5
V major	5-7-9	1-3-5
vi minor	6-8-10	1-♭3-5
vii diminished	7-9-11	1-♭3-♭5

The table above reviews how chords and keys relate to scales. At first recite the degree and quality of each triad as you play its arpeggio ("One major, two minor, three minor, four major," etc.). Then repeat the sequence while reciting the scale degrees (the numbers in the second column), and again while reciting tones in relation to the chord (third column).

Track 64 Diatonic Triad Arpeggios, D major Pattern 1

Track 65 Diatonic Triads in D major

To play the triad arpeggios as chords requires us to move on the fretboard.

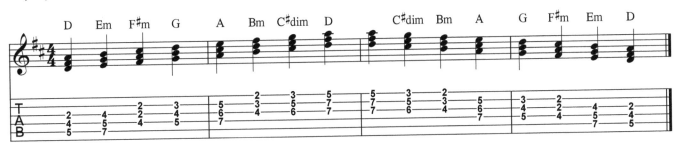

If it's too hard to get through diatonic triads in all five patterns in 5-10 minutes, spread them out and add one per week. Find the pace that is realistic for you.

Track 66 Diatonic Triad Arpeggios, D major Pattern 2

Here are the triad arpeggios in Pattern 2, this time descending from the top note of each on the way up, and ascending from each root on the way down.

Track 67 Diatonic Triad Arpeggios, D major Pattern 3

As an exercise, call out a random scale degree from I to vii and start the arpeggio sequence from there. Here we start on the V of D—A major—and continue with Bm, C#dim, etc.

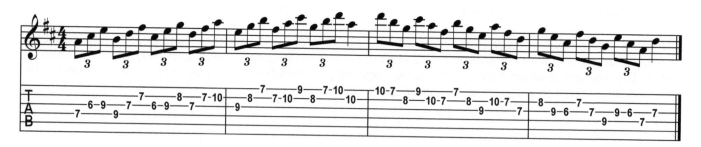

Track 68 First-Inversion Triad Arpeggios

Here we're starting each diatonic triad from its 3rd. Inversion names only specify which is the lowest note. In a close voicing, the root is on the top.

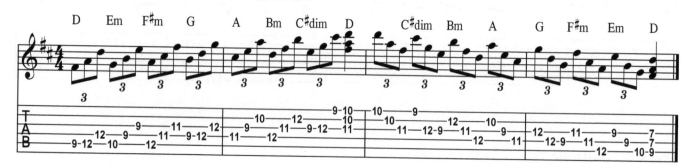

Track 69 Second-Inversion Triad Arpeggios

These have the 5th in the bass, then root and 3rd. Just in case you're playing an acoustic guitar without a cutaway, these are in Pattern 5 of A major so you don't run out of space. But if you can reach up to the 15th fret, then move these up to Pattern 5 of D also.

56

Unit 25: Sweep Picking

To play one note per string on multiple strings in the same direction you can use essentially one big down- or upstroke. The forearm should not make its usual rotation. Instead the wrist is held straight with the palm damping the strings just above the string being picked. The elbow and shoulder move the pick in a straight line, coming to rest against each string before pushing through to play a note and land against the next string.

Most players have an easier time sweeping toward the floor. When sweeping upward, gravity is against you, and maintaining a good pick angle is harder. Try to keep the pick perpendicular to the guitar's face. If the pick flops over too much it makes it hard to change directions. Make sure there's not too much friction where your arm passes over the guitar body.

Notes are fretted, released, and damped by the fretting hand so that only one at a time is sounded. The easiest sweeps are those with one note per string, each fretted by a different finger.

Track 70 Basic Sweep

Sweep technique takes time to master and is hard to keep clean and evenly-timed. Practice very slowly with the metronome, making sure that the last notes of the sweep are the same speed as the first ones, and that you only hear one note ringing at a time. Track your metronome settings from day to day.

Track 71 Sweeps with Shifting

These small sweeps use Pattern 5 triad arpeggios on the top three strings only.

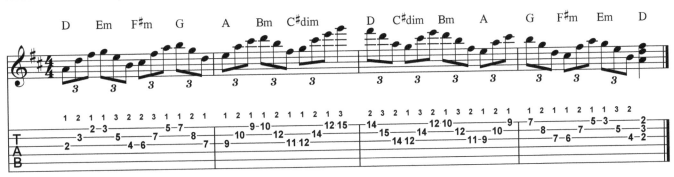

Track 72 Legato and Sweeps with Shifting

This would make a good lick for a modal application like A Mixolydian. Let the pick rest against the next string during the pull-off so the timing is not rushed.

Track 73 String-Skipping Triads

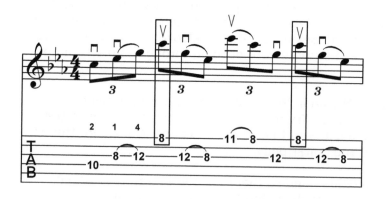

The normal triad arpeggio fingerings can be hard to play at high tempos. Here's a way to play them using economy and outside picking, string skipping, and legato technique. The index finger will be unavailable to damp the 3rd string for the boxed notes. Damp it with the 4th finger instead. This is a root-position Cm triad.

Track 74 Scalar Lines with String-Skipping & Legato

The same approach can work on any scale if you set things up so that you use outside picking when moving from string to string. Economy downstrokes are used when there is no string skip. This example uses the C blues scale.

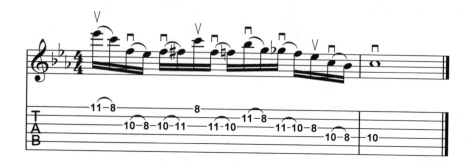

Track 75 More String-Skipping & Legato

This is an excerpt from "Dust Commander" that uses this economical approach.

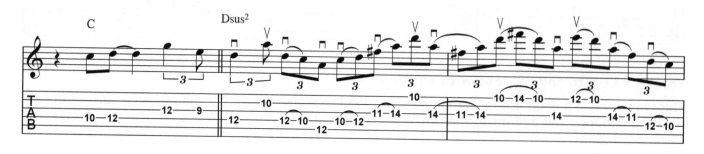

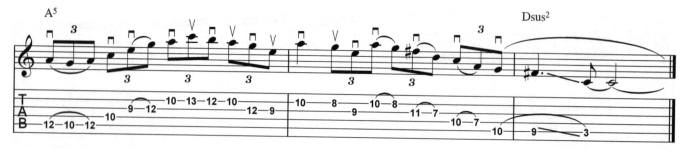

58

Unit 26: Open-Voiced Triads

The previous triads have all been close voicings. In open voicings, we displace at least one note by an octave in either direction. There about ten different possible open triad voicing schemes conventionally available on the guitar; more when you include open strings, two-handed fretting, and harmonics. We're only going to cover single displacements here, but you'll probably want to explore more of them on your own.

First are triads voiced 1-5-3 (1-5-10, to be precise). A notable example of these in use is Eric Johnson's intro to "Cliffs of Dover" at 0:15 (he plays G/B instead of Bm). These can be practiced both as chords and as single-note lines. For chords, hybrid-pick with pinches or strum with the inner string damped. For single-note lines, alternate picking is recommended if the tempo permits, but they also lend themselves to hybrid picking. These are shown ascending only to save space, using Pattern 4, 2, and 5 shapes so that you can play the root with your index finger, but Patterns 1 and 3 are also useful.

Track 76 Open-Voiced Triads in Root Position

Track 77 Open-Voiced Triads with 3rd in the Bass (Voicing 3-1-5)

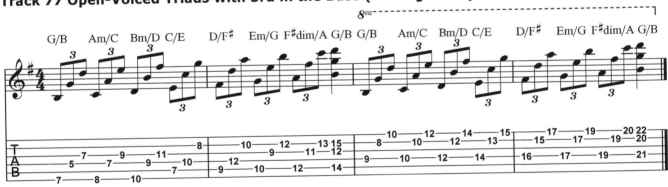

Track 78 Open-Voiced Triads with 5th in the Bass (5-3-1)

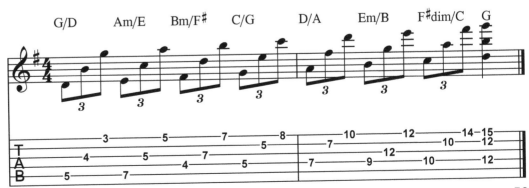

Learn your triads and their arpeggios well, even if your interest is in styles that predominantly use chords of four tones or more. Triads are superimposed over each other to create extended structures and melodic ideas.

More Diatonic 7ths

Another strategy for tough interval skips that works well sometimes is to let your fingers walk into a lower position on the way up, and a higher position on the way down. The previous 7ths example used D Lydian Pattern 3. Here we use the same scale but step from Pattern 4 down to Pattern 3.

Track 79 Walking 7ths

Track 80

This melodic example from "Wrecked on the Sirens' Rocks" uses 7ths in E Mixolydian.

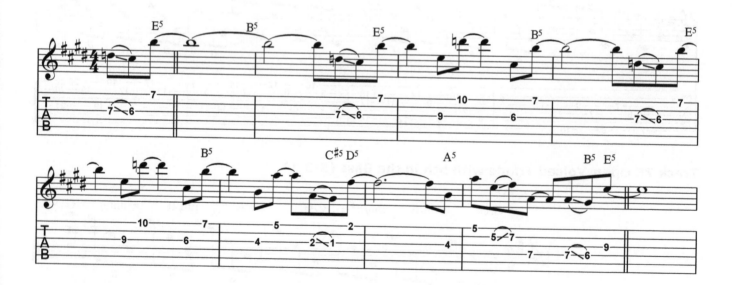

Unit 27: Three-Note Interval Study Matrix

A diatonic triad arpeggio sequence is also a three-note interval study where two consecutive thirds are applied from each scale degree. The result is 1-3-5, 2-4-6, 3-5-7, and so on.

The triads are important because they define chords, but moving to degrees other than 3 and 5 creates new melodic sounds and fingering challenges. Writing out all the three-note permutations within the arbitrary limit of an octave creates an array (or *matrix*) with 64 entries. The triads show up in the gray box in this 2-dimensional array.

1-1-1	1-1-2	1-1-3	1-1-4	1-1-5	1-1-6	1-1-7	1-1-8
1-2-1	1-2-2	1-2-3	1-2-4	1-2-5	1-2-6	1-2-7	1-2-8
1-3-1	1-3-2	1-3-3	1-3-4	1-3-5	1-3-6	1-3-7	1-3-8
1-4-1	1-4-2	1-4-3	1-4-4	1-4-5	1-4-6	1-4-7	1-4-8
1-5-1	1-5-2	1-5-3	1-5-4	1-5-5	1-5-6	1-5-7	1-5-8
1-6-1	1-6-2	1-6-3	1-6-4	1-6-5	1-6-6	1-6-7	1-6-8
1-7-1	1-7-2	1-7-3	1-7-4	1-7-5	1-7-6	1-7-7	1-7-8
1-8-1	1-8-2	1-8-3	1-8-4	1-8-5	1-8-6	1-8-7	1-8-8

Each cell in the table is the starting point of an interval study that you can apply throughout any scale or mode. For example, directly below the triads is the sequence 1-4-5, shown here in A Mixolydian Pattern 5.

Track 81 1-4-5 Sequence, A Mixolydian

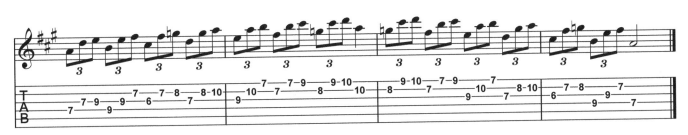

Track 82 Reverse 1-4-5 Sequence, A Mixolydian

The descending part can use the same 3-note sequence as shown above, or you can reverse it. You're learning to find and play the notes you hear in your head, so it's good to work out a way to resolve logically. You could just modify the ending, or plan for the resolution by starting on a specific beat or pitch.

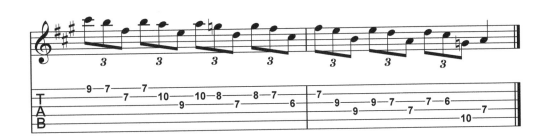

Track 83 1-5-2 Sequence, F Aeolian

Start the exercises from a note in a higher register to help avoid reflexively diving to a low string when it's time to solo. Try starting on any scale degree. Here is the sequence 1-5-2 in F Aeolian Pattern 1, starting from its 2nd, G.

> The existence of matrices in the book does not mean that you have to practice every possible permutation to become a competent player. You could initially try a few boxes at random and pick one to practice that interests you for melodic or technical reasons. Exploring the instrument in this way will build your technique and can spur the creation of a new melody. The cells that repeat the same pitch (1-1-1, 1-1-2, etc.) may seem trivial, but repetition is musically useful and often confusing to the fingers, so don't rule those permutations out.

Triplet Permutations

The studies above only started on the downbeat. Here's the 1-4-5 A Mixolydian example, still in triplets, but phrased as a pickup into each beat.

Track 84 Triplet Displacement 1

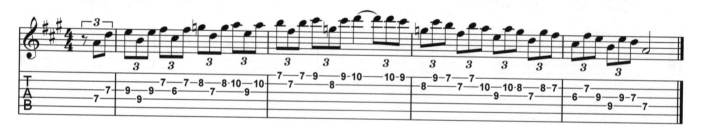

Displacing by another triplet eighth-note gives us the third possible starting timing division.

Track 85 Triplet Displacement 2

Applying the three possible triplet rhythmic starting places to each cell in the table makes 192 permutations.

Straight 8th-Note Rhythmic Permutations

Three-note sequences obviously lend themselves to practice in steady triplets, but we should also make them fit other simple rhythms; for example two straight eighths and a quarter note. Here that rhythm is applied to melodic permutation 1-5-4 in B-flat major, Pattern 3.

Track 86 1-5-4 Sequence, 8th-Note Permutation 1

There are four 8th-note rhythms that contain three attacks within two beats.

Applying these four rhythms to the pitch sequences would create a three-dimensional matrix of 256 possible rhythmic interval studies, starting with:

Track 87 1-1-1 Sequence

and ending with:

Track 87 1-8-8 Sequence

Further rhythmic augmentation of the three notes—across three or more beats—increases the number of permutations exponentially. A common rhythmic figure has attacks on beat 1, the "and" of 2, and the "and" of 3. In the next example it's applied to the sequence 1-5-3 in A minor.

Track 88 1-5-3 Sequence, Dotted Quarter-Quarter-Dotted Quarter

Continue picking hand alternation even when you're not picking to produce the pattern shown.

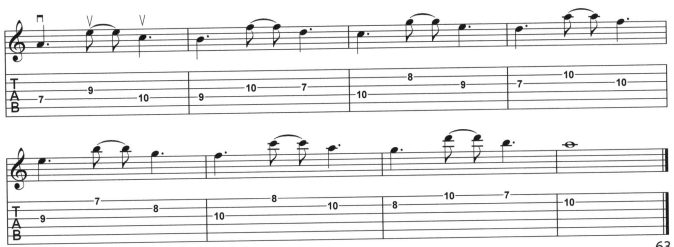

Unit 28: Seventh Arpeggios

Adding another diatonic 3rd on top of each triad gives us 7th chords and their arpeggios.

7th Chords of the Harmonized Major Scale

Degree & Quality	Spelled from Key	Spelled from Its Own Root
I major 7	1-3-5-7	1-3-5-7
ii minor 7	2-4-6-8	1-♭3-5-♭7
iii minor 7	3-5-7-9	1-♭3-5-♭7
IV major 7	4-6-8-10	1-3-5-7
V dominant 7	5-7-9-11	1-3-5-♭7
vi minor 7	6-8-10-12	1-♭3-5-♭7
vii minor 7 ♭5	7-9-11-13	1-♭3-♭5-♭7

Here is one octave of diatonic arpeggios in Pattern 4 of B♭ major. The stock chord shapes over the staff were chosen for playability and do not directly correspond to the arpeggio shapes.

Track 89 Diatonic Seventh Arpeggios, Pattern 4, Root Position

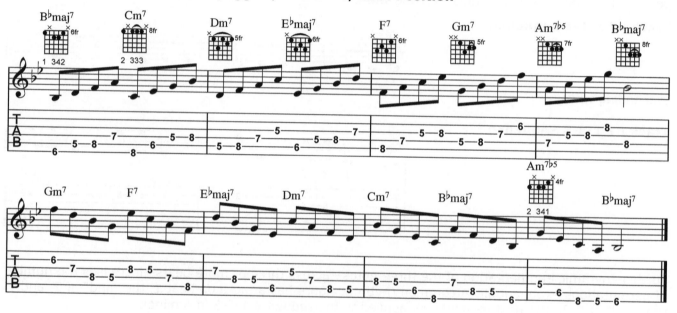

Track 90 Diatonic Seventh Arpeggios, Pattern 4, First Inversion

Here are the same diatonic arpeggios, this time starting from the 3rd of each.

Track 90 continued

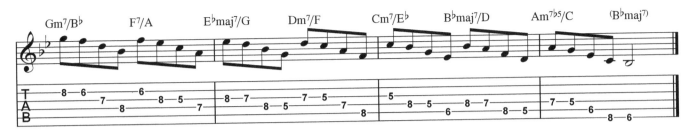

Track 91 Diatonic Seventh Arpeggios, Pattern 4, Second Inversion

Starting from their 5ths.

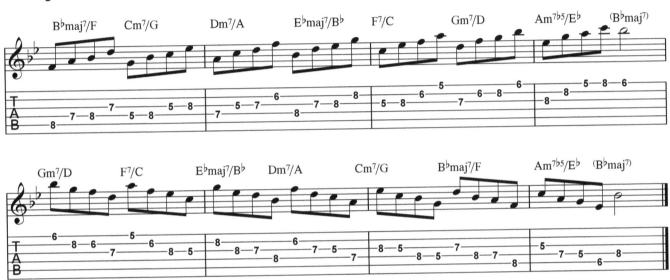

Track 92 Diatonic Seventh Arpeggios, Patterns 4-5, Third Inversion

From their 7ths.

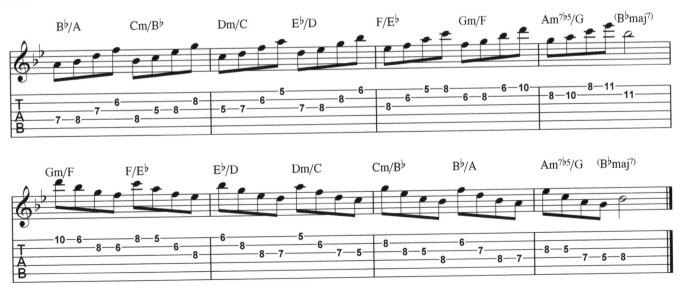

To keep practicing we might move up a 4th and start again with root-position diatonic seventh arpeggios in E♭ major, Pattern 2. As before, the chord shapes must move up the fretboard if you want them to remain uninverted.

Track 93 Seventh Arpeggios, Pattern 2, Root Position

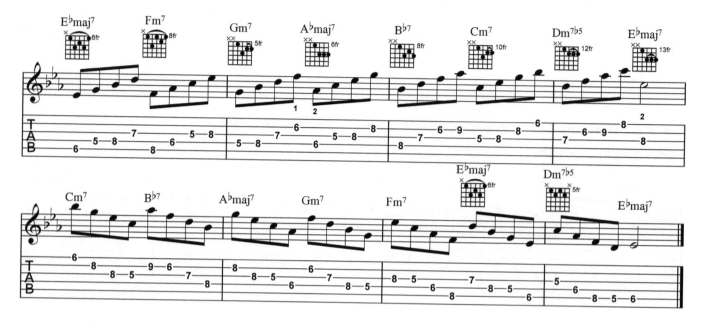

Track 94 Two-Octave Arpeggio

Like the triad arpeggios, 7th arpeggios should be practiced ascending and descending, changing directions, and starting from any chord factor. Here is a B♭maj7 arp starting from its 5th and descending to its 5th two octaves lower before finishing on its root.

Large arpeggio shapes can be sequenced, with each group reflecting a different inversion of the chord. Here's G7 Pattern 4 in descending groups of two from each chord tone.

Track 95 Seventh Arpeggio in Groups of Two

Next we have the same G7 arpeggio in ascending groups of three. The 12/8 time signature can be counted as 4/4. Tap the foot once for each beamed group.

Track 96 Seventh Arpeggio in Groups of Three

Here is a G7 arpeggio in groups of four, with corresponding chord inversions. Inversions are named by the lowest chord factor.

Track 97 Seventh Arpeggio in Groups of Four

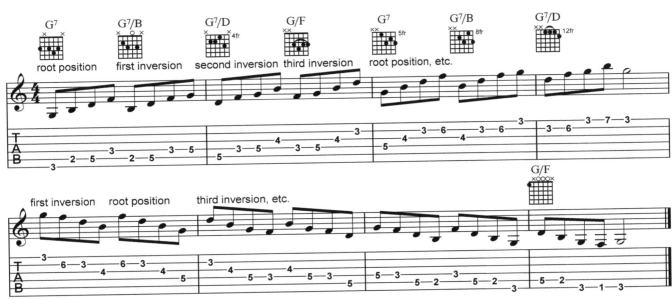

To get started using arpeggios in soloing, concentrate on the top four strings at first, relating them to the chords of the same qualities in the closest available position. The diminished 7th chord and its arpeggio are not diatonic, but useful to include early on.

Track 98 Seventh Arpeggio Types on Top Four Strings, Pattern 4

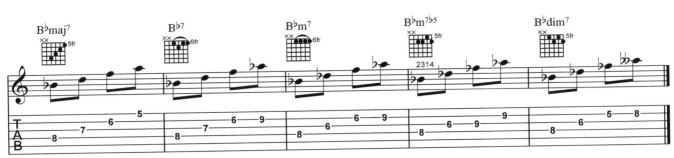

Track 99 Seventh Arpeggio Types on Top Four Strings, Pattern 2

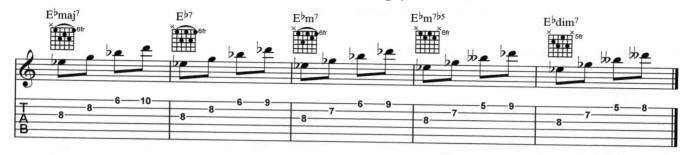

When you can play Pattern 2 & 4 arpeggios without stopping to think, add another pattern. Spread the work out and take your time, but keep going until you have no blank areas on your fingerboard. Remember that smaller pieces (2-, 3-, and 4-note arpeggios) are what you will use most when playing melodically.

Track 100 Arpeggio Phrases

Here are typical arpeggio-based phrases over ii-V-I progressions in F major and E♭ major. The second phrase has cliché chromatic notes on the upbeats after 2 and 4 to set up the tones that follow.

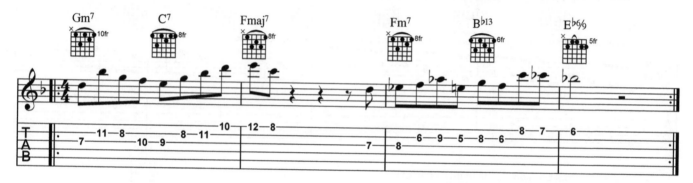

> Scales, arpeggios, and sequences are not music. They are building blocks. Learn and practice them alongside songs and solos by other players, studying phrasing, articulation, rhythm, and harmony.

Unit 29: Four-Note Interval Study Matrix

All the four-note interval studies possible within an octave would create a 3-dimensional matrix with 512 cells: eight tables with eight columns and eight rows each. The first row would look like this:

1-1-1-1	1-1-1-2	1-1-1-3	1-1-1-4	1-1-1-5	1-1-1-6	1-1-1-7	1-1-1-8

and the last row would look like this:

1-8-8-1	1-8-8-2	1-8-8-3	1-8-8-4	1-8-8-5	1-8-8-6	1-8-8-7	1-8-8-8

Now we know we can never run out of new sequences to practice. Going through them systematically or just picking one at random can be a source for new melodic ideas.

To help figure out a new sequence, name the series of intervals created by the degrees in the permutation. Here is an example. For the four-note sequence 1-5-6-4 you ascend by a 5th, then a 2nd, then descend by a 3rd. Play the same series of diatonic intervals from each step to get 2-6-7-5, then 3-7-8-6, and so on. This combination coincidentally spells descending triads with roots on beat 1 or 3.

Track 101 1-5-6-4 Sequence, A major, Pattern 3

Connecting Pentatonics

While playing Pattern 1, visualize Pattern 2 of the same scale, so that you can slide, shift, or stretch into it without a glitch. Playing three notes on any string in a pentatonic pattern moves you into the neighboring one. Shown here are slides between Patterns 1 and 2 of E minor pentatonic, up on string 1 and back down on string 6.

Track 102 Connecting Pentatonic Patterns 1 & 2 on Strings 1 & 6

To continue, practice shifting up on string 2 and down on string 5. When the curved slur marks over the slide marks are not present both notes may be picked—essentially a position shift when executed at higher tempos.

Track 103 Connecting Pentatonic Patterns 1 & 2 on Strings 2 & 5

Keep working through the shifts until you've gone in both directions between the two patterns on every string. A goal is to be able to make the move inaudible whether shifting or stretching to reach the note in the next position.

Work through all the possible adjacent pattern connections:
1-2 and 2-1
2-3 and 3-2
3-4 and 4-3
4-5 and 5-4
5-1 and 1-5

Execute slides cleanly, listening for any open strings or errors in accurate fretting. Keep the same close fretting hand you used for string damping when playing in a stationary position.

Extended Pentatonic Patterns

When you can freely move between any two adjacent patterns, try moving between three or more. One easy pentatonic connection method favored by many players is to play any minor 3rds as string changes. In other words: no three-fret reaches or slides. This restriction produces two extended pentatonic patterns that are easy to finger.

Track 104 A minor or C major Extended Pentatonic

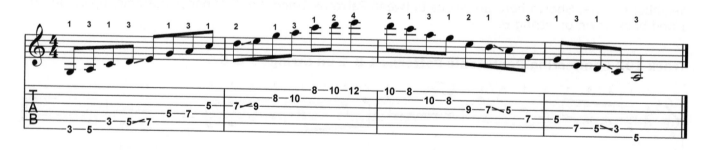

Track 105 E minor or G major Extended Pentatonic

The extended patterns are good starting places for connecting the fretboard (and they're also good for mixing in string bends), but they can limit your expression. Don't stop with them. Work toward making sure you can connect your scale patterns all over the neck so you never get stuck.

The next example traverses all five E minor pentatonic patterns. In addition to shifting, try stretching the fretting hand using the fingering shown. With practice this method can make a smooth-sounding connection. If you're not used to stretching, warm up first, take it very slowly, and pay close attention to how your hand and arm feel. If you notice any pain, however slight, stop and rest. Keep practice of this technique very brief until you're used to it.

Track 106 E minor Pentatonic across the Fretboard

Unit 30: Blues Scales

When you hear the term "blues scale" the one to think of first is the same as minor pentatonic with the one added note, the ♭5. Sometimes the added note is called a ♯4, depending on theoretical or notational considerations. Placing this note between steps 4 and 5 creates two consecutive half steps and a six-tone scale.

Blues Scale

| 1 | m3 | P4 | d5 | P5 | m7 | P8 |

Keep the existing pentatonic patterns in mind as you count and add the ♭5 to each. The patterns shown here are positional. In some licks it works out better to switch the ♭5 to a different string.

D Blues

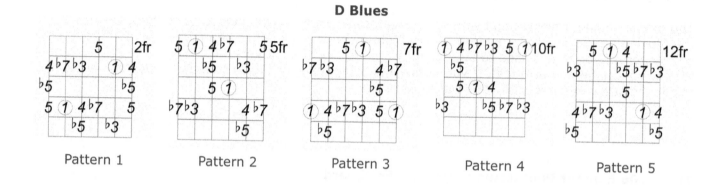

Pattern 1 Pattern 2 Pattern 3 Pattern 4 Pattern 5

Track 107 Blues Scale in Groups of 4

By now you probably know how it would look on paper. Play groups of 4 using all 5 patterns of this scale in 8th notes with the metronome.

Sequencing the blues scale and skipping through it intervallically will help solidify your knowledge and ability to use it. With its two consecutive half-steps this scale will present new fingering challenges.

Track 108 Blues Scale in Descending Groups of Two

Now that you've worked with this book a bit, please post a review. Thanks for your support!

This links to the book at Amazon:

monsterguitars.com/ir

Learn and practice short blues licks (not just from guitarists—piano and sax players have some great ones), and experiment with the scale to make up a few of your own.

Track 109

The Relative or Major Blues Scale

When we studied major and pentatonic scales we learned that the 6th degree of major is the root of its relative minor. Conversely, the 3rd degree of a minor scale is the root of its relative major.

The same applies to the blues scale. An A blues scale (which is essentially minor, though it is often forced over dominant chords and major triads) has the same notes as what we might call a C major blues scale. This scale doesn't have a universally accepted name—you might hear it called *country blues* or *relative blues*. The chromatic note is now the #2 or b3.

Major Blues Scale

1	M2	m3	M3	P5	M6	P8

This scale should not be used over minor chords or minor key centers; just over a I dominant 7th chord or major triad or its related major or dominant-based key center.

Patterns 3 and 4 are good places to play one of the most important bluegrass licks using these notes. Variations of it are used in rock, blues, and jazz, so don't pass it up. When ascending, you want the major 3rd to fall on beat 3. To make this happen, the first note is a quarter note, which forces the next note onto beat 2.

Track 110

73

When playing this phrase use a downstroke on the second note (and alternate-pick in general) to keep the strict 8th-note timing this lick should have when played country style. Tap the predominant beat division with your foot, and keep time in your picking hand, even if the alternating motion is imaginary when you are string-damping and playing long notes, rests, syncopations, slides, hammer-ons or pulloffs.

To extend this lick, we can play it again an octave higher, which is easiest to do by sliding up from Pattern 3 into Pattern 4. On the descending portion, you'd rarely go from the major 3rd straight to the minor 3rd. Those notes are usually kept separate on the way down. Notice how the lick descends to the major 3rd alone, then jumps back up to the 6th, skipping the major 3rd the second time, sliding from ♭3 down to 2 instead.

Track 111 Two-Octave Country Lick

Major Blues Lick Transposition Exercise

Work out two- and four-bar versions of the above phrase in at least 6 different keys, using all five CAGED patterns of the scale. For example, here is how you might play it in F, using Pattern 1 in 5th position, for a phrase that fills two bars but resolves on the downbeat of the next measure.

Here is the same idea in Pattern 2, phrased to fit inside 4 bars.

Unit 31: Three-Note-Per-String Scales

Each of the major scale and mode patterns we learned avoided having two whole steps on the same string.

If we play three notes on every string, besides a slight stretch where two whole steps occur, we also end up with a position shift. Starting on each of the seven unique notes produces seven fingering patterns (continued on next page). When learning and practicing these, it's important as always to remember which notes are the roots and various tones of the major scale or any mode you use the pattern to produce.

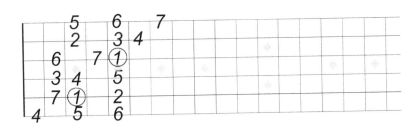

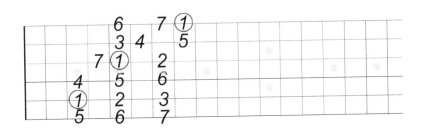

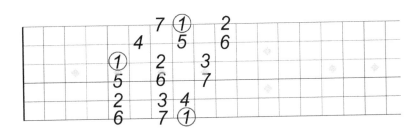

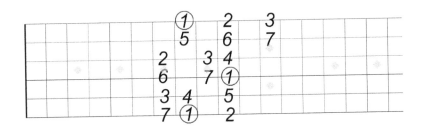

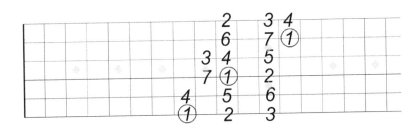

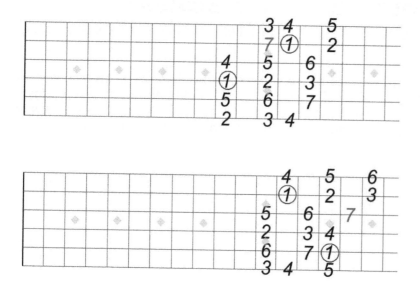

With three-note-per-string patterns, picking directions can become easier; for example down-up-down on each string when ascending. For this sequence first play with regular alternate picking, then try economy-picking the ascending string changes as shown.

Track 112 Three-Note-Per-String Economy Picking

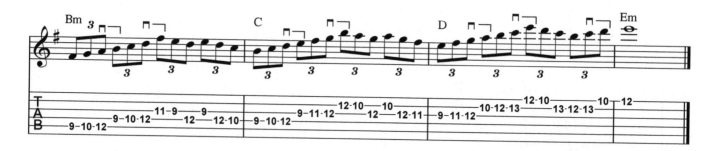

The patterns are good for playing linear phrases, especially if they are rehearsed to fit a particular situation. Here's a lick using 10-note groups and a sweep-picked arpeggio on the ♭VII chord.

Track 113 Three-Note-Per-String E minor Line

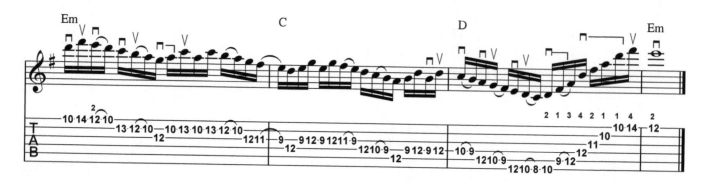

The five positional CAGED-based patterns are easier to relate to the underlying chord shapes, and so may be better for regular melodic playing, improvisation, and rhythm/lead embellishments. There are some fantastic players in all styles, however, who swear by 3-note-per string patterns as the only ones they need for major modes.

Unit 32: Sprint Training

In this section I'm going to write in the first person to emphasize that the topic is speculative.

Much has been written about building speed on the guitar, and it's all good information. The basics of building speed will probably always be: use a metronome and a practice log to track your progress, practice every day without fail, stay relaxed, make sure your technique is clean, strive for accuracy first, and be patient.

However, in sports research a lot of money and effort have been invested and athletes are getting faster all the time, so I decided to try applying some of their concepts, and self-testing. The results were positive, but let me declare in advance that I could not afford to do a scientifically valid study. If one were done it could invalidate or refine the hypothesis that sprint training for sports can transfer to playing an instrument.

It appeared that maybe I had previously taken too long (30 minutes or more) to build up to my top speed in a technical practice session, then tried to play at that highest speed for too long (an additional 60-90 minutes). It could be this is a good regimen for building *stamina* rather than speed. Guitarists need both, but as with athletes, the best sprinter will not beat the best marathoner in his event, and vice versa. Further, even if we need both, it might be best to train them separately.

Besides anaerobic muscle metabolism, sprint training regimens build reflexes, mental focus, and the ability to maintain relaxation and proper technique under demanding conditions.

For this routine, you'll track your tempo with the metronome, playing at your maximum **relaxed** speed for no more than three very short sets, interspersed with 3-5 minute recovery periods of slow playing. Because everything happens in a shorter time frame, it's more important than ever to pay close attention to how your arms and wrists feel, stopping at the first sign of tightness or pain.

1. Warm up carefully at a slow to moderate tempo for about 5 minutes. Practice a lick or passage for which you already have the fingering and picking planned out and memorized.

2. Find your maximum **clean** and **relaxed** tempo for the passage. If you're already into this routine, set your metronome just below the highest tempo you wrote down the day before. Play the passage **one time only** at this tempo.

3. Reduce the metronome to half the tempo and keep playing so that your hands stay warm and loose as you recover from the sprint for 3-5 minutes.

4. If your first sprint was **technically clean** and **relaxed**, try raising the metronome setting slightly above the previous highest setting. If the sprint had any technical problems or was tense, set the metronome slightly **below** the previous high setting. Do your second sprint.

5. After 3-5 minutes of slow playing, do a third sprint, bumping the metronome up again if the second sprint was clean and relaxed, but moving it down if the execution was sloppy or tense.

6. Only repeat the process for a fourth cycle if your tempo continues to increase while your playing is still relaxed and accurate. This is important. As soon as your top speed drops perceptibly at all after the 3rd sprint, **stop** the sprints.

7. Play for another five minutes at half speed to cool down and promote relaxation. Now do some easy unforced hand circles and flexes to help prevent stiffness.

The entire session should only take about 30-40 minutes. The best thing to do now is take a nap so your brain can form its pathways. Don't do the routine again until the next day.

The first time I tried this routine, I was preparing an overdub for "Dust Commander." I had been spending most of my time arranging songs, so my chops were down from a previous high for scalar 16th notes at 170 bpm several years before. Now I didn't have much time. This was going to be economy-picked, but at 178 bpm. I wrote out the part with picking directions, planned for a recording session three weeks away, and started the daily sprint training.

I was tempted to practice for longer sessions, but I'd had plenty of experience telling me that my intuition is often wrong, and the sprint training idea seemed logically sound. I think the routine taught me to use the metronome better as a tracking tool, instead of chasing it. It also taught me that if a recording didn't happen within the first two or three takes, it wouldn't happen at all that day, and I could save money and studio time by just recording something else and trying again another day. I did manage to get a passable take that day, though, so I'm going to keep using this method.

Here's my part. Of course you could use any piece that you want to work up to a high tempo.

Track 114 "Dust Commander" Excerpt

Scales in the CAGED System

It's handy to have these in the back where they're easy to find. Use the pattern number of the root shape to identify all chords, scales and arpeggios.

Major/Ionian. For Mixolydian, lower the 7ths. For Lydian, raise the 4ths.

Major Pentatonic. For "Major Blues," add the ♯2.

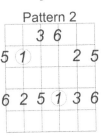 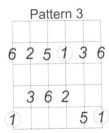 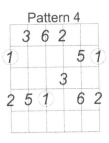

Minor/Aeolian. For Dorian, raise the 6ths. For Phrygian, lower the 2nds.

Minor Pentatonic. For Blues, add the ♭5.

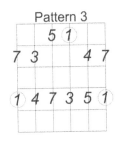 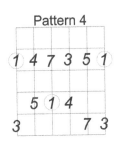

When practicing and performing, "relaxed" means moving with minimal opposing muscle tension, not that you aren't exerting yourself or keeping good posture.

Lightning Source UK Ltd.
Milton Keynes UK
UKHW050734010821
388008UK00005B/123